Basic Techniques of Conducting

Basic Techniques
of Conducting

Kenneth H. Phillips
The University of Iowa

New York   Oxford
Oxford University Press
1997

OXFORD UNIVERSITY PRESS

Oxford   New York

Athens   Auckland   Bangkok   Bogota   Bombay   Buenos Aires
Calcutta   Cape Town   Dar es Salaam   Delhi   Florence   Hong Kong
Istanbul   Karachi   Kuala Lumpur   Madras   Madrid   Melbourne
Mexico City   Nairobi   Paris   Singapore   Taipei   Tokyo   Toronto

and associated companies in

Berlin   Ibadan

Copyright © 1997 by Oxford University Press, Inc.
198 Madison Avenue, New York, New York 10016

Oxford is a registered trademark of Oxford University Press

Library of Congress Cataloging-in-Publication Data

Phillips, Kenneth H. (Kenneth Harold)
Basic techniques of conducting / Kenneth H. Phillips.
p.   cm.
Includes indexes.
ISBN-13 978-0-19-509937-9 (pbk.)

1. Conducting   1. Title
MT85.P52 1997 96-16707
781.45–dc20

19 20 21

Printed in the United States of America
on acid-free paper

This book is dedicated to the memory of my father,

Edwin H. Phillips

(1912–1994),

whose happiest memories were of

those times when he was making music.

Contents

Preface xi

Acknowledgments xv

Lesson 1

The Study of Conducting ■ Class Organization ■ Course
Requirements   1

Lesson 2

Posture and Position ■ Preparatory Gesture ■
Using the Metronome   6

Lesson 3

The Four Pattern ■ Elements of the Pattern ■
Internal and Final Releases   24

Lesson 4

The Four Pattern ■ Varying the Articulation ■
Tempo Terminology   38

Lesson 5

Videotaping #1   45

Lesson 6

The Three Pattern ■ The Two Pattern ■ The Daily Dozen ■
Terminology for Dynamics   49

Lesson 7

Selecting a Baton ■ Dynamic Changes   63

Lesson 8

Baton Grip ■ Character Terminology   67

Lesson 9

Videotaping #2   73

Lesson 10

The One Pattern ■ Midterm Preparation ■ Release on One
■ Accent, Articulation, and Connecting Terms   77

Lesson 11

Release on Beat Two ■ Entrance on a Pickup Note ■
Midterm Preparation   92

Lesson 12

Videotaping #3   105

Lesson 13

Videotaping #4   109

Lesson 14

Midterm Conducting Exam, Part 1   113

Lesson 15

Midterm Conducting Exam, Part 2   117

Lesson 16

Functions of the Left Hand ■ The Circle Drill   119

Lesson 17

Left Hand Sustaining Gestures ■ Coordinating the Two Hands   135

Lesson 18

Left Hand Strengthening Techniques ■ Repeat Markings   147

Lesson 19

Videotaping #5   151

Lesson 20

Subdivision ■ Cues ■ Alto and Tenor Clefs   155

Lesson 21

Composer's Intent ■ Listener's Response   167

Lesson 22

Entrances on Incomplete Beats ■ Instrumental Transpositions:
C and B-flat   170

Lesson 23

Videotaping #6   175

Lesson 24

Fermatas ■ Compound Meters: Six, Nine, Twelve ■
Instrumental Transpositions: F, E-flat, A   179

Lesson 25

Asymmetric Meters: Conducting in Five and Seven ■
Changing Meters   193

Lesson 26

Videotaping #7   197

Lesson 27

Accents ■ Tempo Alterations ■ Section Cues   201

Lesson 28

Conducting Synthesis 1   215

Lesson 29

Conducting Synthesis 2   218

Lesson 30

Videotaping #8   227

Coda   231

Musical Examples Index   233

Topical Index   235

Preface

This is a basic introductory conducting course. It is designed to meet the National Association of Schools of Music requirement that all undergraduate music majors have at least one course in conducting. The course content is appropriate for all music majors, including instrumental, vocal, and composition, and may be used at the graduate level with those who have not studied conducting, or those wishing to review the basic elements.

TO THE STUDENT

The study of conducting is much like the study of an instrument or voice—it is a psychomotor skill acquired over time. As such, the skill of conducting cannot be learned from a textbook. This text can only serve as a guide; your class instructor is the most important source of help. Therefore, regular class attendance is necessary if you are to acquire the information and feedback needed to become a skilled conductor.

This text is organized into thirty lessons, each lesson building upon the last, and each focusing upon a specific technique or techniques which must be practiced in order to become habitual. A good conductor cannot be thinking about conducting technique when trying to lead an ensemble in a meaningful interpretation of music. The conducting gestures must be automatic, and executed in such a way as to convey clear messages to the players or singers. Nevertheless, when learning any psychomotor skill a period of time must be given to mastering the basics before they can be used proficiently. This is the beginning of your "training" period in conducting. Realize that new skills take time to develop; don't become frustrated if initial attempts are not what you want. Daily practice and review of each technique will soon produce the desired results.

All students, whether right or left handed, are encouraged to learn to conduct the basic metric patterns with the right hand. At first this may be stressful for left-handed people, but they will have the advantage when learning to use the left hand for cueing and gestures of expression. Ensemble members, especially at the professional level, tend to expect a certain uniformity in conducting, which right-handed metric patterns and right-handed use of the baton provide.

Unlike many academic courses you may take, where the final grade is based upon cognitive achievement, assessment in conducting is based mainly upon the psychomotor skills you develop. Just as you are evaluated for developing skills in playing an instrument or singing, so in conducting your final grade will reflect more what you can do with what you have learned.

The musical examples in this text are purposely rather easy and uncomplicated. The goal of this conducting method is to build a basic conducting technique upon which you can build your own personal style. Just as everyone must first learn the ABCs before learning to read and write, so a beginning conductor has to learn the basic gestures of the conductor's vocabulary. With music that is rather simple in design, you can more readily concentrate upon mastering the ABCs of effective conducting technique. However, conducting of quality music, no matter how simple, requires expressive communication. From the beginning, make it your goal to become an expressive conductor.

TO THE INSTRUCTOR   The class outline of this course is designed for two hours per week for one semester. The are a total of thirty lessons, one per class session. Longer courses may provide additional time for reviewing the basic fundamentals using the supplemental musical examples provided; the instructor may also want to add additional materials to the course content.

Basic Techniques of Conducting is a competency-based method—that is, specific techniques are introduced, practiced, and evaluated before moving on to the next level of difficulty. Each content lesson introduces the techniques to be mastered and provides Guided Practice outlines for group conducting. An Assignment section at the end of each lesson directs the student in reviewing and practicing and indicates the material to be read and studied for the next class session.

The emphasis of this conducting course is on the psychomotor techniques necessary for clear and expressive conducting. It is my experience that far too often the basic *physical* properties of conducting are minimized in beginning conducting classes; students are expected to conduct movements from symphonies when the basic elements of technique are poorly defined and learned. For this reason, the musical examples in this course have been kept extremely simple; the emphasis is on the gesture. The examples with text may be sung with words or on a neutral syllable. Instrumental parts are provided for most musical examples, and instrumental majors are encouraged to bring their instruments to class, especially for videotaping sessions. If students do not bring instruments to class, they must sing and be an active part of the ensemble.

Ten of the thirty lessons (including the two midterm exam sessions) are designated as videotaping sessions. (Videotaping is an indispensable asset for the teaching of conducting and is available in most schools.) It is during these taping sessions that students are given the opportunity to conduct in front of the ensemble or class as a means of demonstrating mastery of conducting techniques. When the class is relatively small, the instructor may stop after each student conducts to make remarks about what was observed. If the class is large (eighteen students has been found to be the maximum number appropriate for a fifty-minute class), there will be no time for remarks between students. In this case, the instructor may speak quietly on the tape (close to the microphone) as each student is conducting. In either case, when the students view the tape, the remarks will be heard for study and evaluation.

Included in eight of the videotaping lessons is an Evaluation Form for assessment by the instructor and self-evaluation by the students. For the class taping session, the students are to tear out the evaluation form, write their name on it, and submit it to the instructor. The instructor may then shuffle the forms and call the order of names for the taping.

The *grade* section of the Evaluation Form contains space for two markings; the first is given by the instructor for the actual conducting. A system of + (superior), √ (average), and − (poor) has been found to be useful in grading. (The instructor may wish to assign some type of point system to these symbols.) The students are then to view the videotape in the designated location and complete the self-evaluation as explained on the form. When this is returned to the instructor, a second grade (+, √, or −) is given for the thoroughness and accuracy of the self-evaluation. It is recommended that some small part of the course grade be assigned to these eight conducting evaluations, but the greater portion of the final grade should be based upon the midterm and final conducting exams.

Lessons 14 and 15 are the midterm conducting exam, and an evaluation form is provided in Lesson 14. This evaluation is done by the instructor from the videotape. Once the evaluations are returned, students are to view the videotape(s), complete the summary evaluation on the back of the form, and return it to the instructor.

No form is provided for the final conducting exam; this is to be graded on a "global" basis by the instructor, much as a jury grade is given for applied music exams. The content of the final conducting exam is designated, and the instructor should devise a system of grading in which each of the four selections counts for a portion of the final exam grade. As recommended earlier, much of the students' final course grade (as much as 50 percent) should come from the final conducting exam.

No written midterm or final exams are recommended for this course, as I believe that the final grade should reflect achievement in conducting and not cognitive knowledge about conducting. However, the instructor may choose to use written exams and other projects.

Lesson content does contain information about using the metronome, score terminology, and transpositions. Ten quizzes on this information are indicated in the lesson Assignment sections, and the instructor may or may not choose to give such quizzes. I recommend short, ten-point quizzes for motivating students to learn these materials.

The facile uses of alto and tenor clefs and transpositions is not a major objective of this introduction to conducting. Such content is found more commonly in intermediate or instrumental conducting courses. The materials given here are to provide only a theoretical background and are included because many students may never take another conducting course. If there is time, however, and the instructor desires more study of these topics, the instrumental parts for many of the musical examples provide ample opportunity for students to analyze and learn to use clefs and transpositions, as well as the instrumental score.

The course content as presented in this text represents ten years of teaching and refining; the sequence of materials has been carefully studied and matched to the developing needs of the students. Directives are very specific, and some instructors may find them too restrictive. I have found, however, that once a base line is established, students learn to modify and personalize their technique. While no book can teach students to conduct (the instructor being the most important part of the process), it is hoped that the method outlined here will help instructors more readily teach a subject that is often without a clear instructional strategy, and that it will develop a clear and convincing conducting technique upon which students can build their own personal style.

Iowa City *K.H.P.*
September 1996

Acknowledgments

I wish to express my gratitude to the many students in the Techniques of Conducting classes at the University of Iowa who provided the laboratory for developing the sequence of instruction in this book. Thanks also to Randy Aitchison, Shayne Cofer, Steve Emge, Bruce Gleason, Kate Levy, and Jill Sullivan, doctoral teaching assistants, who provided feedback and valuable help in clarifying textual content.

The illustrations in this book are the work of Donald Alvarado, former associate professor in the School of Medicine at Louisiana State University. Photography is by Bruce Drummond, media specialist in the Learning Resource Center of the College of Education at Iowa. Bruce Gleason, a Ph.D. graduate of Iowa, served as model for the photographs.

My gratitude is extended to Maribeth Anderson Payne, my editor at Oxford University Press, for her commitment to this book. It was because of Maribeth's frustrations in a beginning conducting course that the idea was conceived for the production of a textbook that covered the basics, step by step.

Lastly, I express my love and devotion to my wife, Donna. Because of her love and support I have learned that academic accomplishments are not nearly as important as family and service to others. Her life has been a model of loving and caring, and I am among the blessed recipients of both.

■ Basic Techniques of Conducting

The Study of Conducting
Class Organization
Course Requirements

Welcome to the conductor's art. In this first lesson you will be introduced to the following:

- why conducting is an important area of study for all musicians
- the requirements for becoming an accomplished conductor
- the importance of effective communication
- the content and techniques covered in this conducting method
- the importance of daily practice
- class organization and course requirements

THE STUDY OF CONDUCTING

The conducting profession is thought to be a world filled with glamour and recognition. But it is really a world of painstaking preparation and hard work. Those who would make it to the podium are those who recognize the tremendous effort it takes to become a skillful conductor—a master interpreter of music.

You may be studying conducting only because it is a requirement, without any ambition ever to stand before and lead an ensemble. But note this: No study of conducting is ever wasted, for once you understand what it is the conductor is trying to communicate, and how he or she goes about it, you will become a more sensitive and responsive ensemble member. For those of you who become bitten by the conductor's bug, this course will be just the beginning of your preparation for a career in conducting. In any case, this curriculum is designed to introduce you to the fundamentals of conducting. It provides the basis for instrumental and vocal/choral leadership and is intended for students in both areas.

The conductor's art encompasses the whole of music learning. The student of conducting must be a good musician, highly trained in one or more instruments or voice. He or she must have a good knowledge of theory and harmony, musical styles, forms, and performance practices. A conductor must know the literature of various genres and be able to choose wisely in matching the music to the strengths and weaknesses of the ensemble. In short, all of your education in music comes to bear upon what you do as a conductor.

People skills are very important for a conductor. The days of the tyrant are thankfully in the past; people today who would lead must be sensitive and responsive to the needs of others. This is not to say that a conductor can vacillate on musical decisions. While performers in ensembles do not expect to be spoken to as if they had no feelings, they do expect decisive and knowledgeable leadership. A wise conductor knows that people perform better when the ensemble environment is conducive to growth and improvement without the threat of vilification for a mistake. Great music making by an ensemble requires great cooperative effort, and this is best achieved in an atmosphere of mutual respect.

Effective Communication

Perhaps the highest goal for the student of conducting is to learn to become an effective communicator. This involves knowing the music and leading the ensemble in such a manner as to inspire a meaningful performance. No one enjoys attending a concert or recital that is boring and devoid of musical expression. Likewise, no one enjoys singing or playing for a conductor who is satisfied only with a correct rendering of the notes. Musicians in academia often forget that music is more than a cognitive and technical process; great musicians move beyond the notes to convey the subjective meaning and mood inspired by the composer.

Learning to communicate music comes more naturally for some persons than for others; feelings of insecurity often inhibit initial attempts at meaningful expression. Most students have been ensemble members, not leaders, and it takes time to become used to the new role of ensemble conductor. It is important to realize that the nervous "butterfly" feeling is a common experience. Even great artists admit to this condition before a performance, but they do not permit it to affect them negatively. Rather, they interpret this feeling as one of excitement, which motivates them to perform even better. Adrenaline can work for or against you—you must seize the moment and react positively to the challenge of making music happen. As you become more secure at being in front of an ensemble, your ability to communicate effectively will improve.

Mastering the Fundamentals

All effective communication begins with a mastery of the fundamentals of conducting technique. Poor preparation and lack of a clear and commanding technique indicate a conductor who is unconvincing.

The method in this textbook follows a competency-based model in which each technique or gesture must be mastered before the next level of difficulty. The following is a list of the two dozen conducting techniques/gestures to be studied and learned in this course:

1. Posture and physical stance
2. Arm and hand positioning
3. Vertical and horizontal planes
4. Delineation of the ictus (beat)
5. Preparatory gesture and downbeat
6. Rhythmic breathing motion
7. Eye contact

8. Simple metric patterns

9. Delineation of dynamic level, tempo, articulation

10. Internal release and final cutoff

11. Holding and using the baton

12. *Staccato, legato, marcato,* and *tenuto* style

13. *Crescendo, decrescendo,* and *subito* dynamics

14. Entrance on a pickup

15. Ambidextrous and left-hand conducting

16. Cues

17. Sustaining gestures

18. Subdivision and hemiola

19. Entrances on incomplete beats

20. Fermatas

21. Compound metric patterns

22. Asymmetrical metric patterns

23. Accents

24. Tempo alterations

Daily Practice Required

Conducting is a psychomotor skill. It is not something that can be studied the night before the exam with any hope of doing a good job. Just like the practicing of your major instrument, the conducting gesture must be practiced daily if proficiency is to be gained. The patterns must become automatic—that is, you cannot think about where beat two is to be placed while actually conducting music. The technical aspect of conducting must become so thoroughly ingrained that the gestures become natural, reflecting and communicating the musical meaning. **This automatic response requires time and patience to learn, and comes from diligent practice on a daily basis.**

You should practice, when possible, in front of a full-length mirror. At first, this may shatter some delusions about yourself, but soon the practice will be of great help.

CLASS ORGANIZATION

During the first few classes, much time will be spent conducting in unison. After that, assignments will be conducted on an individual basis in front of the class and graded. Students will be videotaped and will be expected to view the videotape outside of class and complete a self-evaluation form as part of the grading process. You will be able to learn a great deal about your conducting by studying the videotape. Your instructor may make comments on the tape itself, which will help to correct conducting problems and aid in the self-evaluation process.

When it is time for you to conduct before the class, step to the podium or conductor's stand with poise and confidence. Be positive in your approach, and remember that initial nervousness is to be expected—don't permit it to defeat you!

One of the greatest problems beginning conductors have is *advertising* their mistakes—they roll their eyes, shake their heads, or heave their shoulders and sigh heavily when something does not work. Or worse, they stop conducting! These practices must be avoided. Every conductor makes mistakes, but the music of an ensemble must not stop because of a conducting error. Good conductors work their way out of a problem, and beginning conductors must learn to do this from the start. Also, reacting to a mistake means that you are thinking about the past, not the future. Conductors are always thinking ahead so as to mentally prepare for that which is to come. Advertising your mistakes conveys a lack of confidence, and conductors must always look confident even when they don't feel confident. There are no perfect conductors; they just don't advertise their mistakes!

It is assumed before a conductor steps to the podium that he or she has thoroughly learned the music to be conducted. You must study the music until you can sing or play every part. Analyze the phrases and the overall structure. Determine what the composer wished to communicate and how this will be reflected in your physical demeanor. The music to be conducted in this introductory course is very simple, for the emphasis is on the gesture, not the music. Nevertheless, even the simplest of musical forms (if it is a valid piece of music) will have something to say to the listener. You must determine *before* you step to the podium how this message will be conveyed by your physical appearance and gesture. Remember that the ultimate goal of a conductor is effective communication.

Because of time limitation, areas of score analysis cannot be dwelt upon in class. However, you can expect assignments in basic nomenclature and terminology, and regular quizzes. These are the areas to be covered: metronome markings, tempo markings, dynamic markings, character markings, connecting terms, repeat sign markings, alto and tenor clefs, C and B-flat transpositions, and F, E-flat, and A transpositions.

COURSE REQUIREMENTS

The following requirements are necessary for the satisfactory completion of this course:

1. Regular attendance
2. Daily practice of assignments
3. Class participation in conducting assignments
4. Successful completion of quizzes, exams, and any projects
5. An open mind to critical evaluation

This last requirement needs some explanation. The process of learning an instrument requires that your instructor provide constant feedback as to your progress. Sometimes this feedback may be rather negative, but when done on a one-on-one basis usually poses no threat. In a conducting class, however, feedback often is given in front of the entire class. When this feedback is negative, some students feel that they are being personally attacked by the instructor. While it is true that instructors should not resort to sarcasm or humiliation as teaching techniques, it is also true that students will make mistakes that need correcting, and this correcting, when done in front of the class, can benefit everyone in the class. Therefore, critical feedback from your instructor must be viewed with an open mind. If you already knew how to conduct, you would not need this class. Remember that the instructor is not criticizing *you* personally, but rather *what* you are doing. Learn to receive criticism as a means to improving, and if a problem arises, make an appointment to speak to the instructor outside of class.

Requirements for the Conductor

The following six requirements are a summary of what it takes to become a good conductor. Keep these in mind and refer to them occasionally as you progress through this course.

1. Good conductors demonstrate musical competence in all areas of study: conducting technique, theory and harmony, sight reading, music history and literature, performance practices, and practical knowledge of the voice and instruments. They also demonstrate broad interests in literature and culture.

2. Good conductors demonstrate leadership in group dynamics—that is, they are able to work well with people and to motivate them. They like people and treat them with dignity.

3. Good conductors demonstrate effective communication and a dramatic flair—that is, they have mastered the art of exaggeration.

4. Good conductors demonstrate competence as educators. Rehearsing involves teaching, and conductors must know how to plan, instruct, model, pace, and create a learning environment.

5. Good conductors demonstrate the organizational skills necessary to manage a music program and successfully meet goals and objectives.

6. Perhaps most important, good conductors love music. Why else would they submit to the long years of training and practice required to become a competent leader? This love of music must come through and be communicated to both the ensemble and the audience. Remember that great music is born in the heart, and from the heart it must flow.

ASSIGNMENT

1. Acquire class text and other materials required by the instructor. In some cases, the instructor may ask you to purchase your own videotapes. (Don't buy a conducting baton until Lesson 7, which will tell you how to purchase the correct style and length suitable for you.)

2. Review the class syllabus and note important videotaping dates when class attendance is essential.

3. Review Lesson 1 and read Lesson 2 for the next class session.

Lesson 2

■ Posture and Position
■ Preparatory Gesture
■ Using the Metronome

Conducting is a physical skill demanding physical preparation. You, the beginning conducting student, must spend much time in learning to physically *prepare* for the act of conducting.

Objectives for this lesson are
- learning the elements of proper conducting posture
- placing vertical and horizontal planes
- positioning the right arm and hand
- establishing and executing the ictus
- executing the preparatory gesture
- using the metronome

POSTURE AND POSITION

The posture of the conductor is of utmost importance in establishing a leadership role. One cannot approach the podium casually; an appearance of authority must be communicated without being overbearing. People are often judged first by their appearance, and this is certainly true of the conductor.

There are six basic elements to good conducting posture. The feet must be flat on the floor (and kept on the floor), approximately six inches apart, with the weight distributed toward the ball of each foot. One foot should be slightly ahead of the other to help prevent the body from swaying side to side. The knees are relaxed and the hips tucked under (buttocks in). The spine is stretched and the sternum (breastbone) elevated. The shoulders are back, down, and relaxed. Finally, the head should be held high with the chin neither lifted nor tucked back (Figure 2.1).

Figure 2.1
Standing Posture

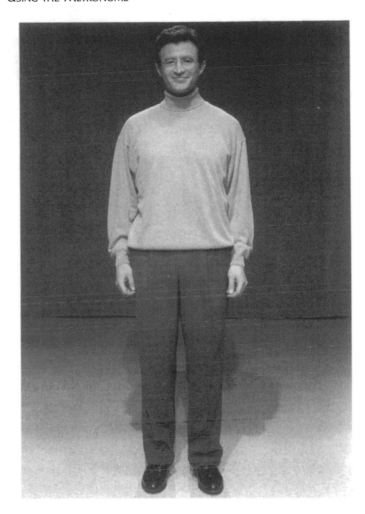

GUIDED PRACTICE*

1. Place your feet approximately six inches apart, with toes pointing forward and left foot slightly ahead of right (Figure 2.2). Lean slightly forward so as to distribute the body's weight on the balls of the feet. Lean backward on your heels and note the danger of losing balance in this position. Place the feet on an equal basis (left foot in line with right foot) and shift the weight from foot to foot. Note the danger of swaying from side to side in this position. Return feet to the first position with the left foot slightly forward; try swaying in this position—it is much more difficult. Maintain a foot position with the left foot slightly forward of the right, the bodily weight forward on both feet, equally distributed. (Left foot forward helps to balance the stance when the right arm/hand extend, drawing the right side forward.)

2. Maintaining the above foot position, lock the knees back and note the discomfort as the legs are tensed and blood flow restricted. Now relax the knees slightly and maintain this position. Note: people often lock their knees when tense; avoid this practice when conducting. Also, avoid relaxing the knees too much, and **do not pulse the beat with either knee or toe.**

---

* The students always stand in a semicircle around the instructor for guided practice.

3. Place the hands over the hipbones with thumbs forward (Figure 2.3). Rotate the hips slightly under by tucking the buttocks in. This helps to straighten the spine and position the abdominal muscles more inward, which is conducive to good posture.

4. Place the palms of the hands together in front of the body in a "praying" position (Figure 2.4). Draw the arms backward, palms out, until they can move no farther, noting the upward stretch of the sternum. Now lower the arms and hands to the sides but maintain a high sternum stretch. An elevated sternum is one of the most important elements of correct posture. Far too many students stand stoop-shouldered and with sunken chests.

5. Roll the shoulders up, backward, and down, as if falling into a groove. The elevated sternum and backward/down positioning of the shoulders work together to maintain an expansive and upright posture. Keep the shoulders *relaxed, slightly back,* and *down.*

6. Elevate the head as if you were being stretched by an imaginary string from the crown. Look from side to side with an ease of motion. Do not stick the chin out or draw it back and inward. Keep the head in a position that is high and floating. Use this guideline: the ears should be over the shoulders, and the shoulders over the hips (Figure 2.5).

7. Form a circle with classmates and walk normally at a slow pace. Now assume an upright and expansive posture, walking "tall" with the weight of the body toward the balls of the feet. On cue from the instructor, return to a normal manner of walking and note how compressed and heel-oriented it is. Return to walking with the upright and expansive posture; this is how one should approach the podium—with vitality and confidence.

8. When turning to face the ensemble on either side, do not be afraid to move the feet in the direction of the turn. Practice turning and taking one step to the left with the left foot, and one step to the right with the right foot. Never cross one foot in front of the other, and avoid "walking around" the podium.

Figure 2.2 Foot Position

Figure 2.3 Hip Roll

Figure 2.4 Sternum Stretch

a. Beginning Position

b. Stretch Position

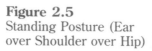

Figure 2.5
Standing Posture (Ear
over Shoulder over Hip)

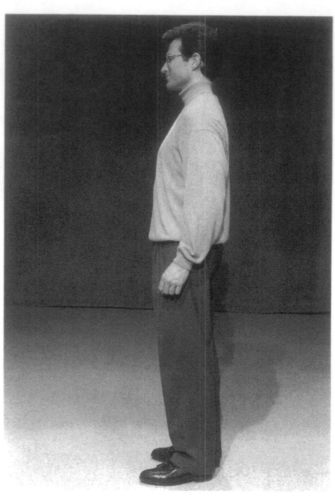

Vertical and Horizontal Planes

Far too many conductors *mirror* everything they conduct—that is, whatever they do with one arm and hand, they do with the other. Therefore, at first, you will learn to conduct with only the right arm/hand, adding the left after the midterm conducting exam. In this way, you will learn the importance of keeping a secure conducting pattern in the right arm/hand, without getting into the habit of mirroring everything with the left.

There are two conducting planes: vertical and horizontal (Figure 2.6). It is upon these planes that the conducting gestures are superimposed. Where the vertical and horizontal planes intersect is the point of the downbeat ictus, or moment the metric pulse is felt. (Some conducting teachers prefer the downbeat ictus to *no!* be placed slightly lower than the horizontal plane. In this text, almost all downbeat ictuses are placed on the horizontal plane. Follow the directive of your instructor.)

The vertical plane for arm/hand positioning may be thought of as an imaginary line extending from top to bottom directly in front of the right shoulder. The horizontal plane is parallel to the floor at about the base of the sternum. The vertical plane extends in front of the shoulder at a comfortable distance (approximately one foot). The horizontal plane extends forward the same distance, but encompasses the area from side to side in front of the torso (Figures 2.7 and 2.8).

Figure 2.6 Positioning of Vertical and Horizontal Planes

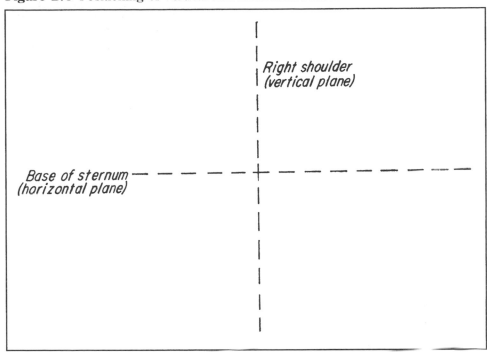

Figure 2.7 Vertical Plane

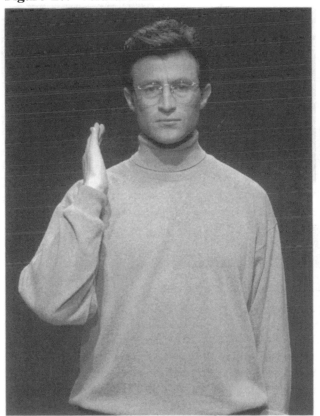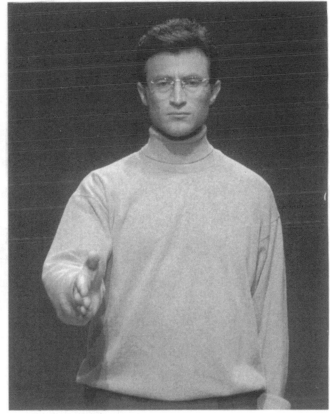

a. Thumb Touching Right Shoulder   b. Right Arm Extended on Vertical Plane

Figure 2.8 Horizontal Plane

a. Thumb Touching Sternum

b. Arm Extended Horizontal to Floor

c. Arm Extended Left on Horizontal Plane

d. Arm Extended Right on Horizontal Plane

GUIDED PRACTICE

1. Extend the right arm and hand in front of the body with the thumb up. Bend the arm upward at the elbow until the thumb touches the shoulder (Figure 2.7). Now lower the arm until it is parallel to the floor. Raise and lower the arm/hand several times to establish the position of the vertical plane in front of the right shoulder.

2. Extend the right arm and hand in front of the right shoulder, parallel to the floor, with palm downward. Move the arm inward (maintaining the parallel position to the floor) until the right thumb touches the chest at approximately the bottom of the sternum (Figure 2.8a,b). Move the arm away from and back toward the body several times to establish the feeling of the horizontal plane. Now extend the right arm/hand approximately one foot in front of the body and glide the arm/hand from left to right and vice versa over this imaginary horizontal plane. Remember to keep the forearm parallel to the floor, and the glide of the horizontal plane parallel to the torso.

3. Return to the vertical plane position and establish its location once again. Drop the arm and hand to the level of the horizontal plane, turn the palm downward, and glide arm/hand across the horizontal plane in front of the body. It is important for you to determine the proper location for each of these planes from the outset (Figure 2.8c,d).

Arm and Hand Position

The correct arm position is extremely important in establishing a clear conducting gesture. The physical components are the shoulder, the upper arm, the elbow, the forearm, the wrist, and the hand. These parts must work together as a unit for effective conducting technique.

The *shoulder* is a ball and joint which serves as a major pivotal point for the movement of the arm. It can lift the entire arm over the head, or it can be used as a stabilizer for other arm movements. Large gestures for loud dynamics require much lifting of the arm from the shoulder socket. However, some conductors develop the annoying habit of conducting everything from the shoulder, with little or no variation to the size of the conducting pattern. This continual arm flapping should be avoided.

The *upper arm* extends outward from the body and slightly forward, as if one were reaching out to shake hands. The *elbow* should be elevated to a position between four and five on an imaginary clock face. Conducting with a dropped elbow restricts motion on the horizontal plane; it is a common problem among beginning conductors. You must learn to keep the elbow elevated for the upper arm to extend out and forward from the body (Figure 2.9).

The *forearm* is attached to the upper arm at the elbow, and this elbow joint must remain free of tension. The forearm should extend in front of the body at an angle with the upper arm of slightly more than ninety degrees. When extended, the forearm must remain parallel to the floor on the horizontal plane. Be careful to keep the elbow up and away from the body.

The *wrist* is important in establishing the precision of the ictus. It must never be rigid, but is more firm for *marcato*-style technique. The wrist at all times should be flexible, but never *floppy*. A waving motion of the wrist blurs the ictus and is to be strictly avoided. Here is a good rule to remember: **The more the arm/shoulder motion, the less the wrist motion, and vice versa.**

The *hand* should be thought of as a natural extension of the arm, and as such is one unit with it. The palm of the hand should usually face downward. The fingers are to be extended in a natural curve when conducting with the hand, and should never be rigid in either a straight-forward or spread position. The thumb rests at the side of the hand against the first finger (Figure 2.10). When conducting on the horizontal plane, the hand must not rotate in such a way that the thumb moves up or down. This will have a negative effect on the conducting plane and the direction of the baton, when it is used.

Figure 2.9 Elbow and Arm Position

a. View from Front

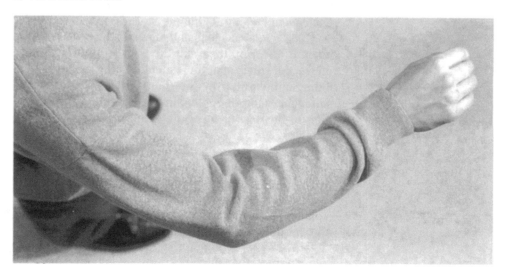

b. View from Overhead

GUIDED PRACTICE

1. Raise the right elbow and arm to a position where the forearm is parallel to the floor and the elbow is between four and five o'clock. Now raise the elbow to a three o'clock position; this position is too high for most conducting. Drop the elbow to the side with the arm extended and try to glide across the horizontal plane. Note the restriction that emanates from the dropped elbow. Return the elbow to a comfortably extended position at the side of the body, between four and five o'clock.

2. With the elbow extended, move the upper arm slightly forward as if reaching out to shake hands. Now extend the arm fully; this rigid position is rarely used in conducting. Draw the arm back too far and note how it pulls the

hand too close to the body. Again, extend the upper arm slightly forward with the elbow gently lifted.

3. With the arm extended in its proper position, look at the angle between the upper arm and forearm; if it is ninety degrees or less it will restrict motion on the horizontal plane. When the hand is extended forward to the vertical plane and the forearm is parallel to the floor, the angle between forearm and upper arm should be slightly greater than ninety degrees, but never straightforward in a rigid manner.

4. With the arm extended in its proper position and the palm of the hand facing downward, extend and curve the fingers naturally with the back of the hand *slightly* higher than the wrist. The thumb rests naturally against or barely touching the side of the first finger.

5. With the arm/hand extended in its proper position, make vertical strokes on the vertical plane with wrist motion only. Now make vertical strokes using the forearm motion from the elbow, keeping the shoulder and wrist joints rather quiet. Finally, make vertical strokes using the full arm by lifting from the shoulder socket. (Do not actually lift the shoulder.) You will need to learn all three of these movements, which are required for different styles of conducting, to be studied later.

Establishing the Ictus

The ictus may be defined as the exact moment the beat occurs. Communicating a clear ictus or beat is central to good conducting technique. In the classical style of conducting, the method taught in this book, the ictus is the point at which the hand or tip of the baton rebounds from the horizontal plane.

It is a common mistake for conductors to blur the exact location of the ictus by failing to delineate its position with a decisive "touching-springing" action of the

Figure 2.10 Hand Position

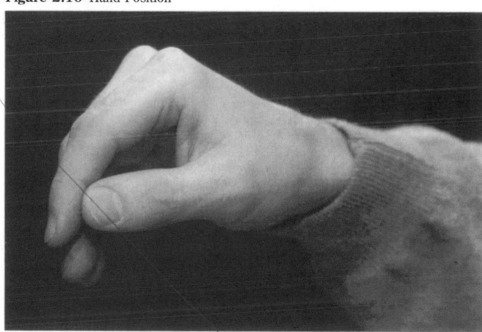

hand/baton. This necessary action is analogous to the motion that one uses to extend and retract a yo-yo on a string (palm facing downward). The feeling is that the hand slightly snaps downward before the hand springs upward. The wrist is important in this action, as it can be neither stiff nor loose. The wrist permits the hand to move slightly downward on the ictus; this motion is immediately countered by a slight elevation of the wrist followed by the upward spring of the hand on the rebound. The spring in the wrist slightly *precedes* the upward movement of the hand and is accompanied by an upward lift of the forearm. Moving only the hand up and down without this unified wrist/arm action will result in a waving hand. At no time should the hand/fingers dip in a dunking fashion. The idea is to place the ictus on the horizontal plane, and the feeling that one wants is that of a slight rhythmic pulse in the wrist/hand.

GUIDED PRACTICE

1. Make vertical strokes (down and up) with the right arm/hand on the vertical plane (directly in front of the right shoulder). Maintain correct arm/hand position; be sure that the elbow is not dropped. Each ictus should occur on the downstroke as it rebounds from an imaginary point on the horizontal plane (arm parallel to floor). Imitate the motion that you would use with a yo-yo. Feel the rhythmic pulse in the wrist/hand as each ictus is delineated and the wrist/arm/hand spring upward.

2. Flatten the top of a music stand and adjust in order for the desk to be at the level where your horizontal plane intersects your vertical plane (Figure 2.11). Make vertical strokes with the right arm/hand on the vertical plane, lightly tapping the top of the music stand for each ictus. The fingertips tap the stand on the downstroke followed by a rebound of the wrist/arm (light lift) and an almost simultaneous springing of the hand/fingers upward. Be careful the hand does not spring up or back too far. The hand must remain a natural extension of the arm. Feel the rhythmic pulse in the wrist/hand as each ictus is delineated. Now remove the music stand and maintain the same feeling and place of the ictus as the vertical stroke rebounds from the imaginary horizontal plane.

PREPARATORY GESTURE

[handwritten margin notes: Gesture / Dynamic - Size / Tempo - Speed / Articulation - Shape / What beat?]

The preparatory gesture is the initial gesture that the conductor gives just before the music begins, and it is one of the most important techniques that a beginning conductor must learn to execute. Failure to learn a clear and decisive preparatory gesture results in ensemble insecurity and lack of precision.

The gesture should send four messages to the ensemble: (1) the dynamic level; (2) the tempo; (3) the articulation style (*legato, staccato, marcato,* etc.); and (4) the preparatory ictus and the downbeat ictus. Most preparatory gestures will start *above* the horizontal plane and to the right of the vertical plane (Figure 2.12).

The height at which the preparatory motion begins is related to the *dynamic level*—that is, the higher the position above the horizontal plane, the louder the dynamic level (Figure 2.13). Shoulder height and above is on the *forte* side, while below shoulder height is the *piano* level. (Some conducting instructors teach that the preparatory gesture begins on the horizontal plane at the place of the first ictus. This gesture does not permit a clear delineation of the character or dynamic level of the preparatory gesture, and is not recommended.)

Figure 2.11
Music Stand Adjusted
for Practice of Beat-One
Placement

The speed at which the preparatory gesture moves sets the *tempo* for the music. This tempo must be set in the conductor's mind *before* the preparatory gesture is given. Failure to do so often results in erratic tempo changes as the conductor works to adjust an original tempo that was prepared incorrectly.

The *articulation* of the music is conveyed by the roundness or angularity of the preparatory gesture. Music that is *legato* will have a greater roundness or curve, while *staccato* and *marcato* styles will be more angular.

Figure 2.12 Positioning of Preparatory Gesture

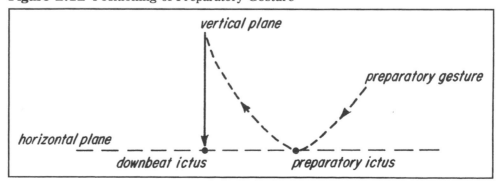

Figure 2.13
Arm/Hand Position for
Preparatory Gesture

a. Position for *Mezzo forte*

b. Position for *Forte*

c. Position for *Mezzo piano*

no! The *preparatory ictus* is always the beat that precedes the ~~downbeat~~ *entrance*. In common time, the preparatory ictus is beat four, for a composition beginning on beat one. In triple time, beat three is the preparatory ictus, and in duple time the preparatory ictus is beat two. One must show this preparatory ictus accurately and in time as it occurs prior to the downbeat ictus. Therefore, the preparatory gesture moves downward to the horizontal plane, rebounds when marking the preparatory ictus, and ends when it moves down the vertical plane to mark the downbeat ictus on which the music begins (Figure 2.12). **The time between the preparatory ictus and the downbeat ictus determines the tempo of the composition.** *- Speed*

Eye contact must be maintained with the ensemble throughout the preparatory gesture and downbeat of the music. A common mistake of beginning conductors is to drop their eyes to the music on the downbeat; this conveys uncertainty and insecurity to the musicians and must be avoided at all times. **Maintain eye contact with the ensemble throughout the preparatory gesture and ~~downbeat~~.** *entrance*

When you step to the podium, you should have your hands to your sides or resting on the stand; your eyes should scan the opening bars of the music. You then mentally set the tempo and confirm the dynamic level and articulation needed; these three elements must be determined and fixed mentally *before* the preparatory gesture is given. Beginning conductors often "jump" into the preparatory gesture without giving thought to tempo, dynamic level, or articulation. The results are usually less than satisfactory. **Prepare yourself mentally before any physical gesture is given. Do not be in a hurry.**

Once the mental conditions are met, raise your right arm and head simultaneously. This signals the group that the music is about to begin. Scan the group to see that all eyes are up and all musicians ready to start. When this is confirmed, give the preparatory gesture. Never lower your eyes before the preparatory gesture once your head is initially raised; this conveys insecurity to the ensemble. **Once your eyes are up, keep them up.**

Breathing with the preparatory gesture is necessary to establish initial rhythmic precision. This *rhythmic breathing motion* is to be used when conducting all groups, even those that do not use breath energy to produce the tone. Drop your jaw sufficiently to convey the initial breath; do not breathe through the nose. Learning to use this rhythmic breathing motion is difficult for beginning conductors, and must be practiced consciously for it to become habitual.

"Prepping the prep" is a fault of some beginning conducting students. In executing the preparatory gesture, they will lift the arm/hand slightly *before* the downward movement of the preparatory gesture begins. This is to be avoided at all times. It sends an incorrect message to the ensemble, and some members may enter early because they will have interpreted the "prep to the prep" as the preparatory gesture. When the preparatory ictus is clearly in the mind as the ictus that directly precedes the downbeat, this faulty gesture will be avoided.

The following is a summary of the techniques needed to execute the proper preparatory gesture:

1. Mentally determine the tempo, dynamic level, and articulation before the gesture is given.

2. Raise the arm/hand and head simultaneously, scan the group for readiness, and keep eye contact throughout the preparatory gesture and downbeat.

3. Raise the arm/hand to a position to the right of the vertical plane, and to the predetermined height to indicate the dynamic level at which the music begins; the higher the louder.

4. Begin the preparatory gesture with a downward movement at the speed of the initial tempo. The shape of this downward movement should correspond to the articulation desired: *legato*, *staccato*, or *marcato*.

5. Breathe simultaneously with the preparatory gesture. Drop the jaw visibly.

6. Indicate the preparatory ictus on the horizontal plane with a rhythmic pulse of the wrist/hand, and rebound to the top of the vertical plane (same height at which the preparatory gesture began).

7. Complete the preparatory gesture with a downward stroke on the vertical plane to the horizontal plane, which is the point of the downbeat ictus.

GUIDED PRACTICE

1. Execute the preparatory gesture a number of times under the direction of the instructor. Assume the proper posture and reestablish the vertical and horizontal planes. Raise the right arm/hand to the right of the vertical plane at approximately shoulder height. Your instructor will set the tempo by counting "1-2-3-4-1," and the preparatory gesture should be given in time so that the preparatory ictus arrives on the horizontal plane on beat "4," rebounds, and continues in tempo to the downstroke downbeat on the last "1." Remember to use a rhythmic breathing motion with the preparatory gesture and to keep the eyes up. (These initial exercises are to be executed in *legato* style with a curved or rounded shape. Different articulation styles will be taught in a later lesson.)

2. Repeat the previous preparatory gesture exercise by varying the tempo and dynamic levels. A *fortissimo* degree of loudness will call for a gesture that starts about eye level, while a *pianissimo* level will begin much closer to the horizontal plane. Your instructor will announce the dynamic level. Set the tempo by counting as above, and be certain to count in a voice level that matches the desired dynamic level.

3. Adjust the music stand desk so as to be level with the horizontal plane. Place the middle of the stand so that it is directly in line with the vertical plane. Repeat the previous preparatory gesture exercise with the preparatory ictus and the downbeat ictus rebounding from the horizontal plane. The preparatory ictus should not fall at the same place as the downbeat ictus; the preparatory ictus should tap the stand to the right of the vertical plane. Focus the preparatory ictus at the right edge of the music stand desk and the downbeat ictus at the center of the music stand. Remember to use a rhythmic breathing motion with each preparatory gesture and to keep your eyes up.

4. Remove the music stand and again practice numerous preparatory gestures at different tempos and dynamic levels. Maintain proper posture, arm/elbow/hand position, and remember to begin the preparatory gesture to the right of the vertical plane and above the horizontal plane. Establish from the beginning the *feel* for your proper vertical and horizontal plane placement. While these initial planes may vary for the music being conducted, they will be used for most of your conducting.

5. Your instructor may check each student individually at this time for proper posture, arm/elbow/hand position, planes, and preparatory gesture. You may be paired with another student to evaluate each other on these initial techniques.

USING THE METRONOME

Every conducting student should have a metronome available for tempo reference. Most contemporary composers will state the metronome marking at the beginning of a composition, for example, ♩ = 60, and the conductor must respect these markings. However, conductors occasionally adjust tempos when the acoustics and/or size and ability of the ensemble demand it.

Some metronomes also list Italian tempo terms, each of which is then represented by a range of metronome settings, for example, *Allegro* = 84 to 144. In this case, the conductor will choose a tempo within this range that best fits the "character" of the composition—lively, dramatic, etc. This is a good rule to remember: The tempo should move no faster than that at which the fastest notes can be executed cleanly and precisely, based on the ability of the group.

Metronome Marking from Tempo Term

Sometimes a composer gives only the Italian tempo and no metronome marking. Use the following two steps to find the metronome setting when only the time signature and the Italian tempo indication are given:

1. Refer to Figure 2.14. Adjacent to the time signature find the note that usually receives one beat in ordinary music. (The slower the tempo, the smaller the note value, and vice versa.)

2. Refer to Figure 2.15. Find the note that usually receives one beat under the Italian tempo term. Adjacent to it is the range of metronome settings, one of which will be chosen for the reasons given above.

Example: What should be the metronome setting for cut time at a tempo marked *allegro*? From Figure 2.14, the half note usually receives the beat. From Figure 2.15, under *allegro*, the half note equals 69 to 112. The conductor should set the metronome within this range, keeping 69 for tranquil, and near 112 for animated moods.

Determining Length

A metronome marking also can be used to determine the approximate length of a composition. Use the following formula for computation:

$$\frac{n \times t}{M}$$

The letters in the formula represent the following figures: n = the number of beats per measure. The t = the total number of measures in the composition. The M refers to the metronome marking itself. A piece of music in triple time (3 beats per mea-

Figure 2.14 Metronome Chart 1: Notes Usually Receiving One Beat

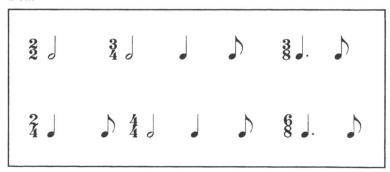

Figure 2.15 Metronome Chart 2: Beat Notes and Metronomic Settings

LARGO	LENTO	ADAGIO
♩ = 42 to 66	♩ = 50 to 66	♩ = 50 to 76
♪ = 48 to 92	♩ = 50 to 69	♪ = 58 to 96
	♩ = 52 to 108	
ANDANTE	MODERATO	ALLEGRO
♩ = 40 to 72	♩ = 60 to 80	♩. = 63 to 96
♩ = 56 to 88	♩ = 66 to 126	♩ = 69 to 112
♪ = 80 to 126		♩. = 72 to 132
		♩ = 84 to 144
VIVACE	PRESTO	
♩. = 60 to 84	♩. = 69 to 120	
♩ = 72 to 92	♩ = 88 to 132	
♩. = 76 to 112	♩ = 96 to 144	
♩ = 80 to 160	♩ = 100 to 152	

sure), of 160 measures in length, and having a metronome marking of ♩ = 90, will last 3 × 160, divided by 90, which equals 5.33 minutes, or 5 minutes and 20 seconds. (Note: to change the hundredths portion of a result to seconds, multiply the hundredths part by 60. In the above example, 33 hundredths × 60 equals 20 seconds.)

GUIDED PRACTICE

Work the following examples to find the length in time of a composition. (Answers appear on the following page.)

1. 50 measures, $\frac{4}{4}$ time, M.M = 60   Time:

2. 200 measures, $\frac{2}{4}$ time, M.M. = 72   Time:

3. 150 measures, $\frac{2}{2}$ time, M.M. = 66   Time:

4. 175 measures, $\frac{3}{4}$ time, M.M. = 62   Time:

Checking Tempo Without a Metronome

Sometimes a metronome is not readily available. To check the tempo of a composition without the use of a metronome, follow these two steps:

1. Divide the metronome marking by 4.

2. Take the resulting number and try to fit that number of counts into 15 seconds by counting aloud. Compare the result to the tempo being used. Increase or decrease the tempo as necessary.

ASSIGNMENT

1. Study Using the Metronome for a quiz on this material in the next class session.

2. Practice the six elements of conducting posture until they begin to feel natural. Observe yourself in a full-length mirror.

3. Maintain the proper arm/elbow/hand position while
    a. making vertical strokes on the vertical plane.
    b. gliding back and forth on the horizontal plane.

4. Practice the "yo-yo" stroke of wrist/arm/hand action while marking the ictus at the intersection of the vertical and horizontal planes. Do you feel the rhythmic pulse in the wrist/hand?

5. Practice giving preparatory gestures using different tempos and dynamic levels. For now, use only *legato* (curved) articulation. Be sure to place both the preparatory ictus and the downbeat ictus on the horizontal plane. The preparatory gesture must start to the right of the vertical plane and above the horizontal plane. Maintain level eye contact and remember to breathe with the preparatory gesture.

6. Read Lesson 3 in preparation for the next class session.

Answers to determining length of a composition:
#1 = 3′ 20″; #2 = 5′ 34″; #3 = 4′ 33″; #4 = 8′ 28″

- ■ The Four Pattern
- ■ Elements of the Pattern
- ■ Internal and Final Releases

Each lesson in this book begins with a review of techniques covered in the previous session.

New skills covered in this lesson are

- ● execution of the four pattern
- ● varying the size of the conducting area
- ● internal and final releases
- ● applying the gestures to music

GUIDED PRACTICE

1. Begin by reviewing the six basic elements of posture. You should be viewed individually for proper conducting stance.

2. Review the elements of arm/hand positioning. You will be monitored individually for the proper arm/hand position.

3. Review the positioning of the vertical and horizontal planes. You are to make vertical strokes down to the horizontal plane and be checked individually.

4. Review the rhythmic pulsing of the ictus through arm/wrist/hand action. Practice this action by making small yo-yo strokes on the vertical plane.

5. Review the elements of the preparatory gesture. Practice preparatory gestures with varying tempos and dynamic levels. Maintain level eye contact and rhythmic breathing motion.

THE FOUR PATTERN

The diagram of the classical four pattern may be seen in Figure 3.1. Notice that all beats occur on the horizontal plane: beat one at the intersection of the planes, beat two to the left of the vertical plane, beat three at an equal distance to the right, and

Figure 3.1 The Classical Four Pattern (*Legato*) (From my perspective)

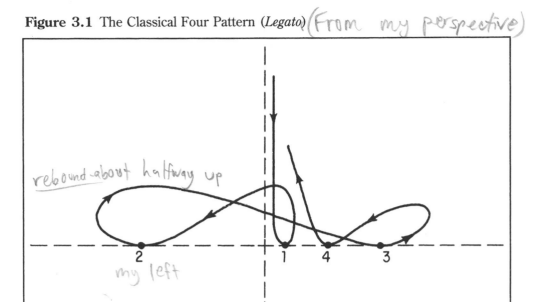

rebound about halfway up

2   1 4   3

my left

beat four to the right of the vertical plane. The pattern that is diagrammed is for *legato* articulation, as the pattern is rounded/curved. The height of the vertical stroke is called the *amplitude*. The width of the horizontal stroke is called the *breadth*.

Notice in Figure 3.1 that the pattern looks somewhat like a figure eight on its side. The loops, however, are not very round but are more oval-shaped, like an egg. The more *legato* the style, the more rounded the loops may become. However, one should guard against making a pattern like the one in Figure 3.2, in which the loops are so large that the pattern becomes confusing and loses its basic form. A good rule to remember: **The rebound motion should never be any higher than half the distance of the vertical stroke.** This will control excessive movement within the pattern of the gesture.

Another common problem when conducting the four pattern is that beat four is often given too high and too far to the right (Figure 3.3). Such a pattern moves the ictus off the horizontal plane and forces the musicians to look up and out on the fourth beat. This is a poor practice, as is placing beat four at the same point as beat one. Beat four must have its own identity, and it should be placed on the horizontal plane slightly to the right of the vertical plane.

Figure 3.2 Incorrect Rebound Loops of the Four Pattern

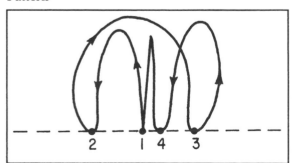

2   1 4   3

Figure 3.3 Incorrect Placement of Beat Four (Common Time)

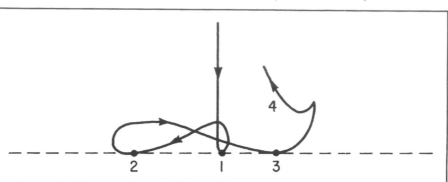

When conducting the four pattern, the arm must be extended sufficiently in front of the body that the left and right motion will not be hindered. Beat two must be placed at an equal distance in front of the body as beat one; beat two should not be drawn back toward the left side of the body.

Executing beat three for beginning conductors is often a problem in that they fail to extend the beat far enough to the right by not extending the forearm (Figure 3.4). This results in a stiff elbow joint. The forearm must open and flow to the right for beat three by increasing the angle at the elbow between the forearm and the upper arm. Also, make certain that beat three *lands* on the horizontal plane.

Another common problem is that beats two and three are placed too close to the vertical plane, thus *bunching up* the beats (Figure 3.5). This confuses the placement of the individual beats and must be avoided. Give plenty of breadth to the placement of beats two and three.

Observe in Figure 3.1 that the rebound motion of beat one lifts to the right before moving left. The rebound of beat two continues slightly to the left before reversing to the right, and the rebound of beat three continues slightly to the right before reversing to the left. You should avoid a rebound that "arches" as in Figure 3.6.

A common error of beginning conductors is that they fail to place all four beats clearly on the horizontal plane. It will take much practice and continued monitoring to develop this habit. You must guard against a vertical plane that wanders off its proper shoulder alignment. The use of a full-length mirror is excellent for viewing conducting planes.

Figure 3.4 Incorrect Placement of Beat Three (Common Time)

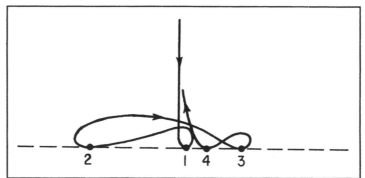

Figure 3.5 Incorrect Bunching of Beats (Common Time)

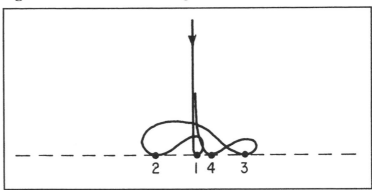

GUIDED PRACTICE

1. Practice the four pattern as guided by your instructor. Begin slowly and gradually increase the tempo to a moderate pace. (If the instructor stands with his or her back to you while modeling, it will help to reduce initial confusion as to the direction of the various beats.)

2. You need to be monitored by the instructor or in pairs for clear execution of the four pattern. Are any of the problems mentioned earlier in evidence? Is the ictus clear for each of the four beats?

3. Combine the four pattern with the preparatory gesture. Your instructor sets the tempo by counting "1-2-3-4-1" with the preparation on beat four. Monitor yourself for eye contact and rhythmic breathing motion.

Varying the Conducting Area

Conducting gestures may be executed in three ways: with the wrist alone, from the elbow/forearm, and with the shoulder/full arm. Conducting with the wrist alone requires flexible and agile use of the wrist joint. It is used for very fast tempos and/or very quiet/soft passages. Much less total conducting area (amplitude and breadth) is covered in this type of gesture.

Most conducting will be done from the elbow/forearm. There is some lift of the elbow (at the shoulder socket) on the rebound of beat four, but most of the motion

Figure 3.6 Incorrect Rebound: Arched

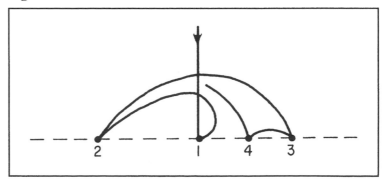

comes from the flexible elbow joint. Both upper arm and forearm move as a unit, and the typical conducting area is covered.

The largest conducting gesture comes from the shoulder and is used for very loud passages, or when the ensemble is so spread out that the breadth and amplitude of the gesture must be increased in order to be seen. When this type of gesture is used, the entire arm/elbow (but not the shoulder itself) is lifted and lowered, with the conducting area being greatly increased. This style of conducting can greatly distract the audience from the music being performed, and its use should be limited.

GUIDED PRACTICE

1. Practice the four pattern by using only the wrist. Note the limited motion that is possible and the restricted conducting area.

2. Practice the four pattern by using the elbow/forearm predominantly. This does not mean that there is no motion of the upper arm or shoulder, but these movements are less extensive than those of the forearm. Be certain to extend the forearm sufficiently to the left and right in front of the body in order that beats two and three are adequately spaced.

3. Practice the four pattern by engaging the shoulder and upper arm extensively. Note the full amplitude and breadth of the pattern.

Varying the Size of the Pattern

The dynamic level of the music being conducted is conveyed by the size of the pattern—the amplitude of the vertical motion and breadth of the horizontal motion. Larger motions are used for loud dynamic levels, and smaller motions for soft dynamic levels. **You must guard against making all dynamic levels look the same in the conducting gesture.**

In general, the amplitude of soft dynamic levels should not rise much higher than the height of the shoulders (unless the entire horizontal plane is raised, as in very soft and light conducting). *Pianissimo* passages will cover the least amount of conducting area.

Loud dynamic levels will be conducted with larger patterns. Be cautious about using too much conducting area, however, as large conducting gestures used continuously desensitize the ensemble to more subtle gestures. The gesture for loud passages should use an amplitude of stroke that goes no higher than the forehead. Very loud passages may take the hand higher, but conducting over the head should be avoided. When a baton is used, it will naturally extend over the head when the hand stops at the hairline. The breadth of the horizontal plane also increases as the dynamic level becomes louder.

GUIDED PRACTICE

1. Conduct four patterns at different dynamic levels. Monitor for changes in breadth and amplitude as dynamic levels change.

2. Combine the preparatory gesture with the four pattern at varying dynamic levels. Note: the preparatory gesture must also reflect the level of the dynamic being conducted. A very loud dynamic level requires a preparatory gesture that starts higher above the horizontal plane than one that is softer.

INTERNAL AND FINAL RELEASES

Internal cutoffs occur within a section or movement, at which time a breath is usually taken or a phrase completed. Final cutoffs occur at the end of a section, movement, or work. Cutoffs must be clearly executed so that no doubt arises in the ensemble as to what is to be done. Most cutoffs include the movement of the left hand. However, for now we will concentrate on the action of the right hand when it is appropriate to use it for a cutoff.

Internal cutoffs, or releases, end with the tail of the cutoff going upward. This is necessary in that the music is not stopping, only pausing ever so briefly, and going on. At a slow tempo, the cutoff may be followed by time for a breath. At a fast tempo, the cutoff and breath are simultaneous.

For now, we will concentrate on the internal cutoff that occurs on beat four. Note in Figure 3.7 that the rebound of beat three lifts more from the horizontal plane, wraps around the vertical plane counterclockwise, and continues up and to the top of the vertical plane, coming to a complete stop on beat four. Observe that the extension of beat three (the "and" of the beat) is the preparation for the cutoff, and communicates to the musicians that a cutoff is forthcoming. This preparation must be large enough to be seen by all of the ensemble members.

A common mistake that beginning conductors make is not stopping clearly on the release. The motion is rounded off at the top before moving down the vertical plane. This is to be avoided. All releases must come to a clear stop, no matter how brief in duration.

The final cutoff or release is diagrammed in Figure 3.8. The preparation for the cutoff is the "and" of beat three; it lifts from the horizontal plane but immediately begins a counterclockwise movement and finishes parallel to the horizontal plane on the right. A final cutoff should end straight out (or with the tail rising only slightly) and with finality. Again, the preparatory loop must be large enough and high enough for all ensemble members to see clearly. The final release is followed by a brief pause before the hand or baton is lowered.

Figure 3.7 Internal Release on Beat Four (Common Time)

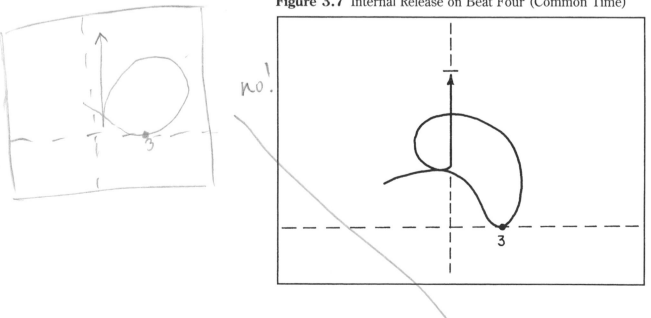

Figure 3.8 Final Release (Cutoff)

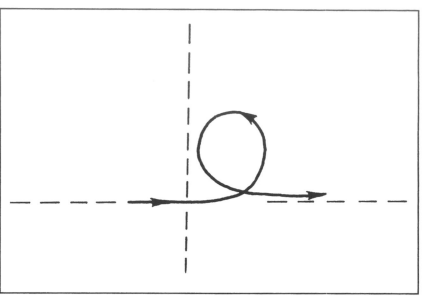

GUIDED PRACTICE

1. Practice the four pattern and execute the internal cutoff on beat four, breathing on the release and continuing on with the pattern. Monitor for a complete stop of the conducting motion on beat four.

2. Practice the four pattern and execute the final release on beat four. Monitor for a complete stop and tail straight out.

3. Practice the four-pattern exercises in Example 3.1 by speaking on a neutral syllable. Note the dynamic levels indicated. Execute internal releases at the places marked with a comma, and final cutoffs at the double bar.

   Note: A clear ictus should be shown for each beat, but when beats are combined into note values greater than a quarter note, then the inclusive beats may be minimized (or melded) after the initial ictus is pulsed.

4. Practice a very *legato* style using the four pattern in Example 3.2 (*Now the Day is Over*). Keep the pattern rather small for the *mezzo-piano* dynamic. Execute internal releases at the places marked with a comma, and a final cutoff at the double bar.

Example 3.1 Four-Pattern Articulation Exercises

Example 3.2 *Now the Day Is Over*

Now the day is o - ver, Night is draw-ing— nigh,—

Shad - ows of the eve - ning Steal a - cross the sky.

Chester by William Billings

William Billings was among America's earliest composers. He was a tanner by trade and a self-taught musician. His composition *Chester* (Examples 3.3 and 3.3a) was popular as a Revolutionary War tune.

Chester is the first piece of music to be studied and conducted individually before the class. As with future compositions, it will be studied by the group, conducted individually before the class for

practice, and then conducted again and videotaped for evaluation.

Chester contains four 4-measure phrases. The character of the piece is "with strength" and requires a rather decisive ictus. The tempo is M.M. ♩ = 120, and the dynamic level is *forte*. The meter is in four. There is an internal release at the end of each of the first three phrases, and a final cutoff at the conclusion of the piece.

Example 3.3 *Chester*

Example 3.3a Instrumental Parts for *Chester*

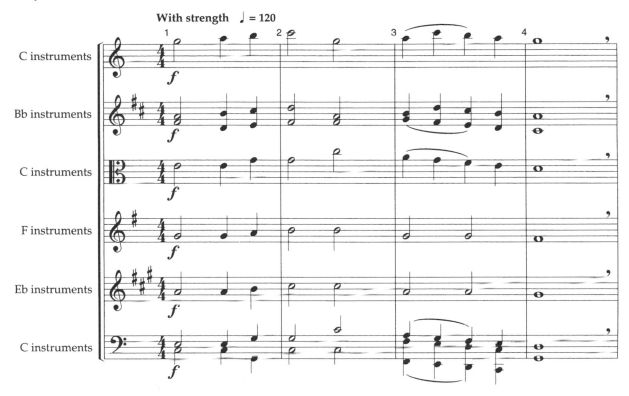

GUIDED PRACTICE

1. Observe your instructor conducting *Chester.* This process should serve as a model for your own conducting.

2. Practice conducting *Chester* in unison. Monitor for a preparatory gesture that looks strong, begins high enough for *forte,* and clearly marks the preparatory ictus. Be certain to use rhythmic breathing motion for the preparation and at each release (except the final cutoff). The instructor will set the tempo by counting as before.

Austrian Hymn by Franz Joseph Haydn (supplemental example)

This famous tune was written by Haydn and is found in two of his compositions. When Haydn was commissioned to write a hymn for the birthday of Emperor Francis II in 1797, he wrote the tune and words ("Gott! erhalte Franz den Kaiser") for the *Emperor's Hymn* (or *Austrian Hymn*). Haydn was very fond of this short composition, playing it several times shortly before his death. It is characteristic of his gift for writing simple but beautiful melody in the Classical style. Haydn used the theme as the basis for a set of variations in the slow movement of his *String Quartet,* Op. 76, No. 3, "Emperor." For many years the tune served as Austria's national anthem. Today, the music, set with other words, serves as the German national anthem.

The version used here (Examples 3.4, 3.4a) is an adaptation from Haydn's original score, with English words. Like *Chester,* it should be conducted with strength and a rather marked four pattern.

Example 3.4 *Austrian Hymn*

Glo - rious things of thee are spo - ken, Zi - on cit - y of our God;

God, whose word can - not be bro - ken, Formed thee for a blest a - bode.

On the rock of a - ges found - ed, What can shake thy sure re - pose?

With sal - va - tion's walls sur - round - ed, Thou may'st smile at all thy foes.

GUIDED PRACTICE

1. If class time permits, the instructor will model the conducting of *Austrian Hymn,* with students observing the process. (If class time does not permit, this composition may be studied for presentation as a substitute for *Chester.*)

2. If *Austrian Hymn* is used, practice conducting it in unison. Monitor for a preparatory gesture that looks strong, starts high enough for *forte,* and clearly marks the preparatory ictus. Be certain to use rhythmic breathing motion for the preparation and at each release (except the final cutoff). The instructor will set the tempo by counting as before. Note the internal cutoffs as marked by commas.

Example 3.4a Instrumental Parts for *Austrian Hymn*

ASSIGNMENT

1. Continue to practice all elements of posture, arm positioning, vertical and horizontal planes, and preparatory gestures.

2. Practice the four pattern at various tempos and dynamic levels.

3. Review and conduct Examples 3.1 and 3.2.

4. Practice *Chester* and/or *Austrian Hymn* with internal and final releases. Use a full-length mirror to monitor your conducting.

5. Read Lesson 4 in preparation for the next class session.

Lesson 4

- ■ The Four Pattern
- ■ Varying the Articulation
- ■ Tempo Terminology

The review process is an important one, as is observing the model of your instructor. When possible, you should observe and be observed by other students.

In this lesson you will learn to
- refine conducting of the four pattern
- conduct *legato, staccato,* and *marcato* styles
- apply appropriate gestures to musical examples
- recognize Italian tempo terminology

GUIDED PRACTICE

1. Review the basic elements of posture, the right arm/hand position, and the placement of the vertical and horizontal planes.

2. Practice preparatory gestures with varying tempos and dynamic levels. Maintain level eye contact and rhythmic breathing motion.

3. Practice the four pattern, placing each ictus on the horizontal plane with a decisive pulse of the wrist/hand. Monitor for equal placement from the vertical plane of beats two and three, and a beat four that is to the right of beat one. Control for excessive rebound motion.

4. Practice varying the size of the conducting area by conducting only with the wrist, then the forearm, and finally the full arm. Combine these areas with varying dynamic levels, *pp* to *ff*.

5. Review the elements of the internal and final releases (cutoffs). Practice these releases alternately using the patterns in Example 3.1. Monitor for a complete stop/break, and tail flat on the horizontal plane for the final cutoff.

Figure 4.1 *Legato* Articulation

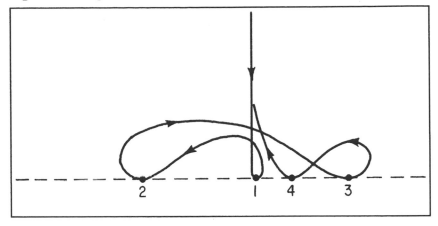

VARYING THE ARTICULATION

We have seen that the conducting gesture communicates four important elements: ictus, dynamic level, tempo, and articulation (*legato, staccato, marcato*). Articulation is shown in the rebound portion of the conducting gesture—the movement from one ictus to the next.

Legato articulation is communicated by rounded rebound motions that flow in a curvelike fashion from beat to beat (Figure 4.1). The larger the loop or curve of the rebound, the more *legato* the articulation. One must be careful, however, not to obscure the ictus by so much "flow" of the rebound that the ictus becomes unclear. Even in very *legato* music, an ictus must be present.

Staccato articulation is communicated by angular rebound motions that move in a quick, "checkmark" fashion from beat to beat (Figure 4.2). In softer/lighter music, this motion comes from a wrist action that springs or snaps on the ictus. While *staccato* articulation is rare at the *forte* level, it does occur. The wrist gesture must then combine with a greater use of the forearm. Note: the wrist must not be too loose; it must also have a sense of snap or spring for *staccato*.

Marcato articulation is communicated by deep angular rebound motions that move in decisive, accented fashion (Figure 4.3). There is almost no wrist action, as wrist and arm become unified. A moment of complete stop follows the quick snap of the rebound before the gesture moves quickly to the next ictus. Showing *mar-*

Figure 4.2 *Staccato* Articulation

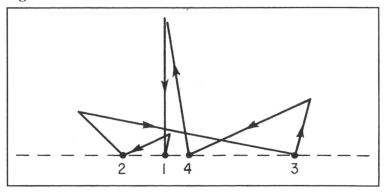

Figure 4.3 *Marcato* Articulation

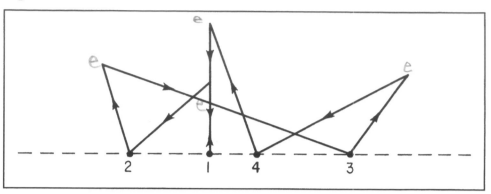

cato accents requires space between each ictus; this is accomplished by the momentary stop or pause of the rebound action between beats.

All rebound motions, whether for *legato, staccato,* or *marcato,* continue in the same direction. The rebound of beat one lifts upward before changing direction. In the four pattern, the rebound of beat two continues to the left before reversing direction, and the rebound of beat three continues to the right. The rebound of the last beat moves upward to prepare for the next downbeat. It is the character or shape of the rebound that determines the nature of the articulation, not the direction.

GUIDED PRACTICE

1. Practice the four pattern with varying styles of articulation: *legato, staccato,* and *marcato.* For a very *legato* style, feel as if the arm/hand is flowing through water, with the water providing a certain resistance to the movement of the gesture.

2. Practice the four pattern with varying styles of articulation and dynamic levels. For very fast, soft, and *staccato* music, the horizontal plane is often elevated so as to depict a "lightness" in the gesture. One rarely finds music that is soft and *marcato,* but such a gesture should be practiced for future reference.

3. Practice the exercises in Example 4.1 by speaking the rhythms (and articulations) on a neutral syllable. Note the dynamic level and tempo indications. Execute internal releases at the places marked with a comma, and final cutoffs at the double bars.

4. Practice the introduction to the "March" from *The Love for Three Oranges* by Prokofiev (Example 4.2). This rhythmically active tune has a built-in *staccato* quality with additional heavy accents. Use the full-arm gesture to communicate the *fortissimo* dynamic, and a sharp flick of the wrist to indicate the *staccato/marcato* articulation.

5. Practice the theme of "In the Hall of the Mountain King" from *Peer Gynt Suite No. 1* by Grieg (Example 4.3). The melody is first stated very soft and *staccato* in the lower strings. Use mostly wrist action with very little forearm movement; more forearm movement may be added for the accents.

6. Review conducting *Chester* by Billings (Example 3.3) with a rather "marked" articulation. Show a strong ictus on each quarter-note pulse, while deemphasizing or "melding" the following beats on notes longer than a quarter in

duration. Monitor each other in pairs; one half of the class sings/plays as the other half conducts to the partner. Your instructor will set the tempo by counting aloud so that all students begin together. Monitor for a strong ictus and beats that are well spaced on the horizontal plane.

7. Review conducting *Austrian Hymn* by Haydn (Example 3.4) with a firm but flowing *legato* articulation. Feel as if the arm/hand is meeting some resistance as it flows through the four pattern (as if conducting under water). Remember to communicate strength of line by standing tall with the sternum elevated.

Example 4.1 Four-pattern Articulation Exercises

Example 4.2 "March" Theme from *The Love for Three Oranges*

Example 4.3 Theme from "In the Hall of the Mountain King"

TEMPO TERMINOLOGY

Words indicating tempo are often given in Italian, regardless of the native language of the composer or publisher. All of the terms are relative and have evolved into a traditionally ranked order. The terms given below are from fast to slow.

Terms Indicating a Fixed Tempo

Italian	English
Prestissimo	As fast as possible
Presto	Very fast
Allegro	Fast, quickly
Allegretto	Moderately fast
Moderato	Moderately paced
Andantino	Moderately slow
Andante	Slow but moving
Adagio/Lento	Slow
Larghetto	Very slow but moving
Largo	Very slow and broad
Grave	Very slow and heavy

Terms Indicating Variations in Tempo

Ritardando	Gradually slower
Rallentando	Gradually slower and broader
Ritenudo	Suddenly slower
Allargando	Gradually slower and louder
Calando	Gradually slower and softer
Sostenuto	Sustaining
Accelerando	Gradually faster
Stringendo	Gradually faster and hastening
Piu allegro	More lively
Piu mosso	More motion
Meno mosso	Less motion
Morendo	Dying away
Tempo rubato	Taken freely
A piacere	At pleasure
Tempo giusto	In exact tempo
Alla misura	Strict tempo
Senza misura	Freely
A tempo	Previous tempo (used after one of the above variations)
Tempo primo	First tempo
L'istesso tempo	Same tempo (beat remains the same even though the meter changes)

Notice that modifying words have different effects on the tempo words, depending on the meaning and translation. *Andante molto,* for example, translates literally as "moving much" and means faster than *andante. Adagio molto* means "slow much," therefore slower than *adagio.* Likewise, *meno allegro* means "less fast," therefore slower than *allegro,* while *meno adagio* means "less slow," therefore faster.

A similar arrangement is true of the diminutive forms of some tempo words. *Allegretto,* for example, meaning "little allegro," is slower than *allegro,* while *adagietto* ("little adagio") is faster than *adagio.*

ASSIGNMENT

1. Study Tempo Terminology for a quiz on this material in the next class session.
2. Practice all elements of posture, arm positioning, vertical and horizontal planes, preparatory gesture, and the four pattern.
3. Practice the four pattern with varying styles of articulation. Review the exercises in Examples 4.1, 4.2, and 4.3.
4. Practice *Chester* (and/or *Austrian Hymn*) for presentation in the next class session. **This will be the first videotaping.**
5. Read the introduction to Lesson 5 in preparation for the next class session. Review Evaluation Form I, which will be used in conjunction with the videotaping.

■ Videotaping #1

Today is the first day that you will conduct in front of the class.

In this lesson you will be expected to demonstrate

- correct conducting posture and arm/hand positioning
- preparation set and execution of the preparatory gesture
- eye contact and rhythmic breathing motion
- clear execution of the four pattern within the vertical and horizontal planes
- proper dynamic level and articulation
- internal and final releases
- communication of "strength" while conducting

Preparation

Remember from Lesson 1 that initial nervousness is to be expected; it is how you *channel* these feelings that makes the difference. Assume a confident and positive demeanor; confidence grows by *doing,* and by midterm you will feel more relaxed and in control. **Remember: Do not advertise your mistakes!**

Read the elements that will be evaluated in this first videotaping as found on Evaluation Form I in this lesson. This will serve as a good review of all gestures and techniques studied thus far. Follow the directives as to the use of the form once you have viewed the videotape of yourself conducting. Your instructor will make constructive comments on the tape, which will help you to complete the self-evaluation form.

For the videotaping, the instructor will collect the evaluation forms and call the names at random. Students will conduct in that order.

When your name is called, proceed to the conductor's stand, place your music on it, and fix the tempo in your mind *before* raising your head and arm. Once you are set to begin, raise your head and arm simultaneously, scan the group with your eyes, give the preparatory gesture with rhythmic breathing motion, and keep your eyes up on the downbeat. *Chester* and *Austrian Hymn* are so simple that you should have the music memorized; use it only for a reference. When you have finished,

everyone applauds to commend you for your courage! Bow appropriately to ac-
knowledge this response.

If something goes wrong with your conducting at the very beginning, stop and
begin again (call a "let" ball); initial nervousness will sometimes cause a bad start.
If, however, you lose your place or the pattern falters during the music—keep going! You must find a way to the end if only by giving a series of downbeats.

Lastly, try to communicate a feeling of strength (stand tall) as you conduct *Chester*
or *Austrian Hymn*. No matter how good your technique is, you will be unconvincing if you do not convey *strength* in your physical demeanor.

When it is someone else's turn to conduct, be a good ensemble member. Respond
to the person conducting, sing or play out, and follow the tempo given. Hold your
music up and maintain eye contact. Do not practice your conducting while seated;
this confuses the conductor and shows that you are not actively participating as an
ensemble member. Remember the old saying, "Rome was not built in a day."
Learning to conduct takes time, and you will make mistakes at first no matter how
much you practice. Give yourself time, practice daily, and you will improve.

GUIDED PRACTICE

> 1. Warm up by group practice of *Chester* and/or *Austrian Hymn*.
>
> 2. Ask your instructor any last-minute questions at this point before the video-
>   taping begins.

VIDEOTAPING #1— *CHESTER* (Billings) AND/OR *AUSTRIAN HYMN* (Haydn)

ASSIGNMENT

1. View Videotaping #1 in the designated location. Complete Evaluation Form I on
   both sides and turn it in to the instructor on the designated day.

2. Continue to practice all conducting elements.

3. Read Lesson 6 in preparation for the next class session.

Name _____ Date ____/____/____ □□
Grades

EVALUATION FORM I

View the videotape of your conducting. Listen to the instructor's comments and complete the self-evaluation below. Leave those elements blank that are basically correct; use + for very good elements and − for those that need improvement. You will receive two grades on this evaluation: the first for your actual conducting and the second for the accurate and timely completion of this form. Do not lose this form.

Posture—Arm/Hand Positioning

_____ proper foot position	_____ upper arm forward
_____ knees relaxed	_____ elbow lifted
_____ straight spine	_____ forearm—upper arm angle
_____ sternum up	_____ forearm extended
_____ shoulders back/down	_____ proper hand position
_____ head high	_____ fingers naturally curved

Preparation

_____ mental set	_____ correct tempo
_____ group scan	_____ correct dynamic level
_____ smooth preparatory gesture	_____ correct articulation
_____ rhythmic breathing motion	_____ clear ictus
_____ eye contact	_____ confident and assuring demeanor

Four Pattern and Releases

_____ vertical plane location	_____ pattern clarity
_____ vertical plane amplitude	_____ internal releases
_____ horizontal plane location	_____ final release
_____ horizontal breadth	_____ release preparation
_____ clear ictus on each beat	_____ communication

Evaluation Summary. On the back of this evaluation form, summarize your conducting evaluation in narrative form. Write one paragraph summarizing the positive elements of your conducting and one paragraph on those elements that need improving. Respond also to your *feelings* about this first conducting experience.

47

Summarize positive elements:

Summarize those elements in need of improvement:

- The Three Pattern
- The Two Pattern
- The Daily Dozen
- Terminology for Dynamics

Learning to conduct well requires constant review. Not until techniques studied previously have been mastered and become habitual can new techniques be mastered.

The new techniques to be learned in this lesson are
- the three and two patterns
- the Daily Dozen
- application of new techniques to musical examples
- terminology for dynamics

THE THREE PATTERN

The classical outline of the three pattern is shown in Figure 6.1. Notice in this pattern that beat two moves to the same point as beat three in the four pattern. Beat three in this new pattern is positioned at the same point on the horizontal plane as beat four in the four pattern.

Two common problems occur in executing the three pattern. Beat two does not extend far enough to the right (Figure 6.2), and beat three does not make contact

Figure 6.1
The Three Pattern (*Legato*)

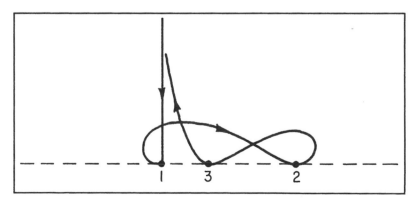

Figure 6.2
Incorrect Placement
of Beat Two

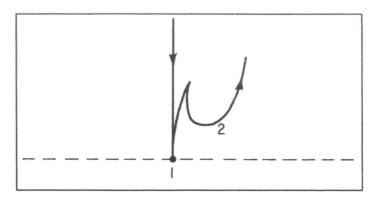

with the horizontal plane (Figure 6.3). The forearm must extend to the right and the angle at the elbow must open sufficiently to permit beat two to flow to the right. Beat three must be lowered to the horizontal plane before rebounding.

GUIDED PRACTICE

1. While the instructor models the three pattern, practice this new pattern a number of times. Divide into pairs to monitor each other.

2. Practice conducting the three pattern with wrist motion only, from the forearm, and with the whole arm.

THE TWO PATTERN

The classical outline of the two pattern is shown in Figure 6.4. Notice in this pattern that beat one moves to a point slightly lower than the horizontal plane, and beat two is placed on the horizontal plane. This exception to the rule for beat one is necessary for pattern clarity; it enables beat two to be placed sufficiently close to the vertical plane without confusing it with beat one. Beginning conductors sometimes reverse the rebound of beat one, causing it to move to the left. The rebound of beat one must move to the right.

All patterns will vary according to the tempo, articulation, and dynamic level. The two pattern shown in Figure 6.5 may be used when the tempo is very fast and there is little time for rebound motion. It is executed with the wrist movement only and uses little or no motion of the forearm or upper arm.

Figure 6.3
Incorrect Place-
ment of Beat Three

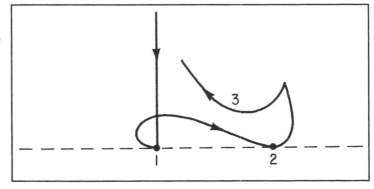

Figure 6.4
The Two Pattern
(*Legato*)

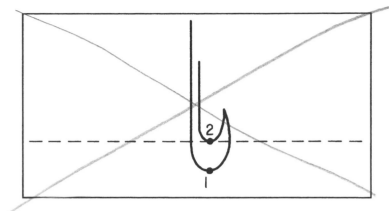

Figure 6.5
Two Pattern: Fast
Tempo

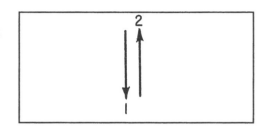

The two pattern as shown in Figure 6.6 is more angular and is suited to *staccato* articulation. Notice that there is very little rebound of beat one. Most of the motion will come from snapping the wrist, but some forearm movement also is required.

The two pattern as shown in Figure 6.7 is very angular and works well for *marcato* articulation. Notice the deep V of the rebound. Remember that *marcato* articulation requires a brief stopping of the motion following the rebound. The full arm motion typically is used when conducting *marcato*.

Figure 6.6 Two Pattern: *Staccato*   **Figure 6.7** Two Pattern: *Marcato*

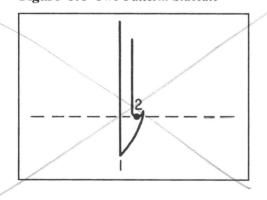
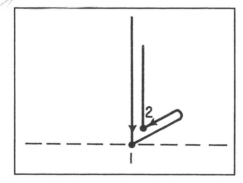

GUIDED PRACTICE

1. Observe the instructor modeling the two pattern, and practice this new pattern a number of times. Divide into pairs and monitor each other.

2. Practice conducting the two pattern with wrist motion only, from the forearm, and with the whole arm.

3. Practice the exercises in Example 6.1 by speaking on a neutral syllable. Note the meter, articulation, tempo, and dynamic level for each exercise.

4. Practice the opening theme from the second movement of Beethoven's *Symphony No. 7 in A Major,* Op. 92 (Example 6.2). Notice that the two pattern uses both sustained (*legato*) and *staccato* articulation, as well as *portato,* a sustained but detached *legato.* Try to indicate this change in articulation with subtle wrist movement (small flicks or checks) for the *staccato* and *portato* styles.

5. Practice "Hornpipe" from *Water Music* by Handel (Example 6.3). This lively piece moves in a quick and bouncy three. In the absence of instruments, singers can perform this example in the key of A major on "du."

Example 6.1 Practice Patterns in Triple and Duple Meters

Legato ♩ = 72   *mezzo forte*

Staccato ♩ = 94   *piano*

Marcato ♩ = 60   *forte*

Example 6.2 Theme from *Symphony No. 7*, Movement 2

Example 6.3 "Hornpipe" from *Water Music*

THE DAILY DOZEN

The Daily Dozen exercise involves conducting the two, three, and four patterns in that order, four times each, for a total of twelve executions. Before conducting each set of twelve patterns, choose a tempo, a dynamic level, and an articulation. For example, one set could be conducted at a fast tempo, medium soft, *legato*. The next set might be slow, medium loud, *marcato*. Conduct no more than six sets of twelve at each practice interval. The right arm tires quickly for beginning conductors; shake the arm liberally after each set to reduce tension.

Daily practice of the two, three, and four patterns is a necessity if these patterns are to become automatic. The Daily Dozen exercise should now be added to your daily practice as a basic means of warming up and habitual pattern execution.

GUIDED PRACTICE

1. Observe the instructor as he or she models the Daily Dozen exercise, counting aloud each of the patterns: "1-2, 2-2, 3-2, 4-2; 1-2-3, 2-2-3, 3-2-3, 4-2-3; 1-2-3-4, 2-2-3-4, 3-2-3-4, 4-2-3-4."

2. Practice the Daily Dozen, following the lead of the instructor, who will announce a dynamic level and articulation for each set. The tempo may be given by counting aloud: "1-2, 1-begin." Note: It is sometimes helpful for beginning conductors if the instructor says "switch" on the last beat of a pattern before changing to the new pattern. This cues the students that the change to the new pattern is occurring. This verbal cue may be dropped as students become familiar with the exercise.

My Country, 'Tis of Thee (Anonymous)

Practice *My Country, 'Tis of Thee* (Example 6.4) in preparation for individual conducting before the class. The meter is in three, the tempo is moderato, the dynamic level is *mezzo forte,* and the articulation is *legato.* The preparatory gesture is the same as that given for the four pattern, except that the preparatory ictus now becomes beat three.

Internal releases occur in measures six and ten, with a final release on beat three at the end. The internal release on beat three is diagrammed in Figure 6.8. Notice that the rebound of beat two moves counterclockwise and wraps around the

vertical plane before ascending the vertical plane. This motion positions the gesture for the downbeat of the next phrase. As for all internal cutoffs, there must be a complete break in the motion to signal the breath and release, which in this case are simultaneous.

The final cutoff on beat three is diagrammed in Figure 6.9. The rebound of beat two again moves counterclockwise, but this time completes the circle with the final tail extending to the right on the horizontal plane. The final release must come to a complete stop, and the conductor should pause briefly before lowering the arm/hand/baton.

Example 6.4 *My Country, 'Tis of Thee*

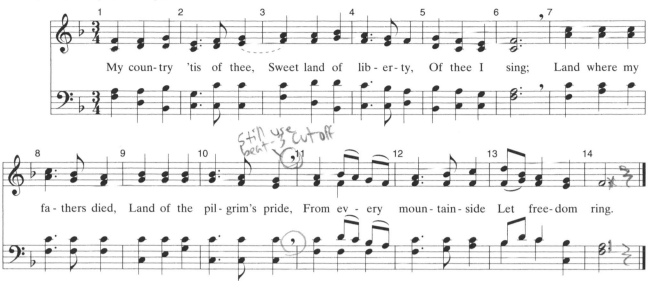

Figure 6.8
Internal Release on
Beat Three

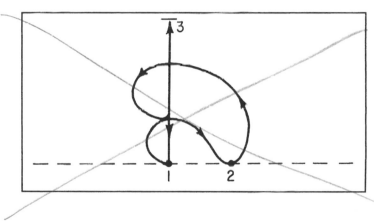

Figure 6.9
Final Release on Beat
Three

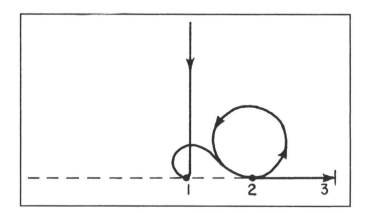

Example 6.4a Instrumental Parts for *My Country, 'Tis of Thee*

"Ode to Joy" from *Symphony No. 9 in D Minor* by Ludwig van Beethoven

The Choral Finale, "Ode to Joy," from the fourth movement of Beethoven's *Symphony No. 9 in D Minor*, Op. 125 (Example 6.5), contains one of the world's most famous melodies. You will conduct it in the next videotaping (Lesson 9). The meter is duple, the tempo *allegro: asai vivace* (♩. = 84), and the dynamic level is *forte*. This highly spirited piece requires a rather marked conducting gesture, which conveys the "joy" intended by the composer and Schiller, the poet.

Example 6.5 "Ode to Joy" from *Symphony No. 9*, Movement 4

Example 6.5a Instrumental Parts for "Ode to Joy"

Internal releases occur at measures eight and sixteen, and a final release occurs at the end. The internal release on the last part of beat one is diagrammed in Figure 6.10. Notice that the rebound of beat one continues in a counterclockwise movement around the vertical plane, stops at the bottom of the circle to indicate the cutoff on the eighth rest, then ascends the vertical plane for beat two and the breath. Again,

a clean break must occur in the motion to indicate the cutoff before beat two (breath).

The final release on two in duple meter is diagrammed in Figure 6.11. The rebound of beat one again moves counterclockwise, but continues to the right on the horizontal plane. The tail of final cutoffs should not rise, but must remain parallel to the horizontal plane.

Figure 6.10
Internal
Release on
Beat Two

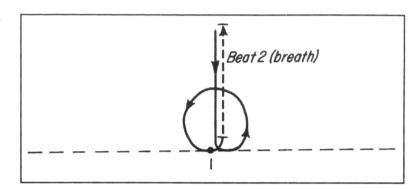

Figure 6.11
Final Release on
Beat Two

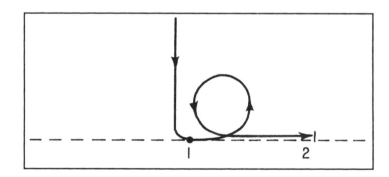

TERMINOLOGY FOR DYNAMICS

Terminology for degrees of loudness and softness is often given in Italian. As with the tempo terms, dynamics are relative and must be adjusted to the size of the ensemble and the acoustics of the performance hall. The modifying Italian word *piu* ("more"), when applied to *piano* and *forte,* should be translated literally so that *piu piano* means softer, and *piu forte* means louder.

Terms Indicating a Stable Degree of Volume

Italian	Abbreviation	English
Pianissimo	*pp*	Very soft
Piano	*p*	Soft
Mezzo piano	*mp*	Moderately soft
Mezzo forte	*mf*	Moderately loud
Forte	*f*	Loud
Fortissimo	*ff*	Very loud

Terms Indicating a Change in Volume

Forte-piano	*fp*	Loudly-softly
Sforzando	*sfz.*	Loudly accented
Crescendo	*cresc.*	Becoming louder
Decrescendo	*decresc.*	Becoming softer
Diminuendo	*dim.*	Diminishing
Crescendo poco a poco	*cresc. poco a poco*	Louder little by little
Subito piano	*sub. p*	Suddenly soft
Subito forte	*sub. f*	Suddenly loud
Crescendo molto	*cresc. molto*	Becoming much louder
Crescendo e diminuendo	*cresc. e dim.*	Gradually louder, then gradually softer

ASSIGNMENT

1. Study Terminology for Dynamics for the next quiz.
2. Practice the Daily Dozen exercise, varying the tempo, dynamics, and articulation.
3. Practice *My Country, 'Tis of Thee* in triple meter and "Ode to Joy" in duple meter. Monitor for the preparatory gesture as to tempo, dynamics, and articulation.
4. Read Lesson 7 in preparation for the next class session.

■ Selecting a Baton
■ Dynamic Changes

Thus far you have been conducting without a baton, but music that is organized metrically is much clearer if a baton is used to execute the basic metric pattern.

In this lesson you will learn to
- select the correct baton for your use
- refine conducting of the two, three, and four patterns
- vary the size of the pattern according to dynamic changes

SELECTING A BATON

You will need a conducting baton for the next class session. Before you purchase one, here are some guidelines to influence the style you choose.

The best conducting batons are made of wood and can be quite expensive. Beginning students are encouraged to purchase fiberglass batons, as they are relatively inexpensive and more durable.

It is very important to match the length of the baton to your physical shape. Standard baton lengths are ten, twelve, and fourteen inches. The majority of conductors can use the twelve-inch baton. When the baton is held in the right hand, the handle points to the palm, and the shaft points at an angle so as to bring the tip to the center of your body. This creates a new vertical plane for the baton (center-line of the body), but the right hand must remain in the position of its vertical plane (in front of the shoulder).

When purchasing a baton, experiment with various sizes to determine what length best suits you. Conductors with long arms often are able to use longer batons, while those with shorter arms may need shorter ones.

The size of your torso also influences the length of the baton. When experimenting, remember to use good arm positioning, and keep the elbow up and extended. If the baton is positioned correctly, it will angle slightly to the left and the tip will be directly at the center (button line of shirt/blouse) of the body. Your instructor will check to make sure you have chosen the correct size, but initial understanding of baton size may save you from having to exchange it.

One other characteristic of the baton is very important—the handle. Large, long handles (often made of cork) should be avoided, especially for people with small hands. This type of handle is often held under the fingers because it is too long to maintain in the palm of the hand. This may result in a baton angle that is too far left and a compensatory action by the wrist that makes the wrist look unnatural. Also, a long handle tends to be held with too much grip, which reduces the subtle response action needed in conducting.

Small, ball-like handles may encourage too much wrist action and require that the baton be held primarily on the shaft. While this type of handle is fairly common, it lacks the flexibility needed to vary the conducting articulation.

The best type of handle is made of rubber or wood, approximately two inches in length and rather small in diameter. It is good, although not necessary, if it tapers naturally to the shaft.

A good baton should be light in weight and well balanced, so that it can lie across the upturned palm of the hand without falling to the floor. Batons that are too heavy and too long lack the flexibility needed for varying the conducting gesture.

GUIDED PRACTICE

1. Practice in unison several sets of Daily Dozens. Monitor for correct placement of all beats on the horizontal plane.

2. Take turns leading the class in a Daily Dozen. The tempo is to be set by saying "1-2, 1-begin." (To save time, state the tempo, dynamic level and articulation for each set.) Offer comments as to how each student is executing the three patterns.

DYNAMIC CHANGES

Two common dynamic changes are the *crescendo* and *decrescendo*. The *crescendo* may be shown by increasing the size (amplitude and breadth) of the pattern, and the *decrescendo* may be shown by decreasing the size of the pattern. While it is common to use the left hand to indicate such dynamic changes, the size of the pattern in the right arm/hand also must vary according to the level of dynamic change.

The *crescendo* seems to be more easily shown by beginning conductors than the *decrescendo*. The weakness in the latter occurs when the size of the pattern is decreased too quickly. Work for a subtle change in the gesture (becoming smaller) as the dynamic level decreases.

Sudden dynamic changes as in *subito forte* and *subito piano* also must be shown in the conducting pattern. Preparation for such a change to louder or softer needs to start on the beat just prior to the dynamic change. For example, in a four pattern, a dynamic level of soft becoming suddenly louder on a downbeat would necessitate that beat four prior to that downbeat be shown at the same dynamic level as the *forte* section. In this way, the conductor prepares the ensemble for the change that is to happen. Waiting to change the size of the pattern to match exactly the time when the sudden dynamic changes occurs is too late, and will not bring about the desired musical results. **Conducting is the art of preparation.**

GUIDED PRACTICE

1. Practice two, three, and four patterns while conducting *crescendo-decrescendo* dynamic changes. Vary the number of measures for this exercise from two to four to eight.

2. Practice the exercises in Example 7.1 by speaking on a neutral syllable. Be sure to vary the dynamic levels of the voice.

3. Practice the theme in Example 7.2 from Dvořák's *Slavonic Dance No. 10,* Op. 72, No. 2. Vary the size of the conducting pattern to represent the *crescendo* and *decrescendo* as shown.

4. Practice in unison both *My Country, 'Tis of Thee* (in three) and "Ode to Joy" (in two). Monitor for correct pattern size and articulation.

5. If time permits, volunteers may conduct the class in either of the two examples above.

Example 7.1 Pattern Exercises for Dynamic Changes

Example 7.2 Theme from *Slavonic Dance No. 10*

ASSIGNMENT

1. Secure a baton for the next class session. Follow the guidelines as given at the beginning of this lesson.
2. Continue practice of the Daily Dozens.
3. Continue practice of *My Country, 'Tis of Thee* and "Ode to Joy."
4. Practice the dynamics exercises in Examples 7.1 and 7.2.
5. Read Lesson 8 in preparation for the next class session.

Lesson 8

- ## Baton Grip
- ## Character Terminology

Be sure that you have secured a baton for this lesson.

Objectives for this lesson are
- mastering the basic baton grip
- learning to use the baton for basic patterns
- character terminology

BATON GRIP

There are numerous possible grips for using the baton. Only the standard grip is taught here, as it is one of the most flexible for all styles of conducting.

Hold the baton in the right hand by gripping it lightly between the pad of the thumb and first joint of the forefinger, at the point where the handle joins the shaft (Figure 8.1). Notice that the forefinger makes a slight U shape. If the handle is tapered, both thumb and forefinger will grip it, but if the handle is not tapered, the forefinger will come to rest more on the shaft. This gives a certain stability to the baton. The remaining fingers should curve gently inward; never should they stick straight out.

The handle of the baton points to the palm of the hand, and does not lie under the fingers (Figure 8.2). In this position, the shaft will angle slightly to the left from the arm/hand position. This should place the tip of the baton at the center of the body, which is the vertical plane for the baton (Figure 8.3). The direction of the shaft may be changed slightly by sliding the thumb forward or backward, and by adjusting the handle in the palm of the hand through contact with the curved fingers.

Only two points of contact with the baton (thumb and forefinger), as in Figure 8.1, are necessary for a flexible conducting style. *Marcato* conducting requires a firmer grip; the handle is grasped by all fingers in a more closed fashion (Figure 8.4). For a lighter, open, *legato* style, two points of contact are sufficient (thumb and forefinger) with the remaining fingers slightly extended.

The baton must be thought of as an extension of the arm, with the ictus transferred to the tip of the baton. For this reason, the tip of the baton must lower to the

Figure 8.1 Standard Baton Grip

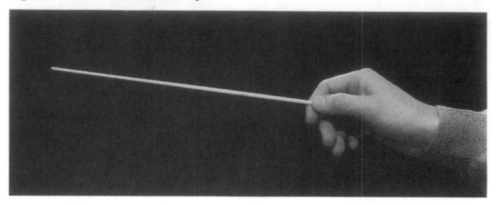

horizontal plane, placing each ictus on it. Many conductors fail to lower the baton sufficiently, thus presenting a double ictus—one at the level of the hand and a higher one at the level of the baton tip (Figure 8.5). Such conducting is confusing and must be guarded against at all times.

To keep the ictus at the baton tip, keep the palm of your hand downward, and lower the forearm to the horizontal plane. If the under part of the forearm can be seen at the completion of the downward stroke, the baton will be higher than your hand. Also, do not rotate the wrist so that the thumb moves upward; this will cause the tip of the baton to elevate to a position higher than the hand. And do not swing your hand from side to side (thumb up, thumb down) when moving across the horizontal plane; this will elevate the baton and cause a false ictus.

Besides the double ictus, other problems can arise when using a baton. When moving to the left, as on beat two in the four pattern, some conductors "slice" the air with a whiplash-type motion toward the body. This moves the ictus from the horizontal plane and all but hides it from the right side of the ensemble. This can be corrected by keeping the baton as a natural, forward extension of the arm, thus not permitting the baton to change angles as it moves left.

Figure 8.2 Baton Handle Pointing into Palm of Hand

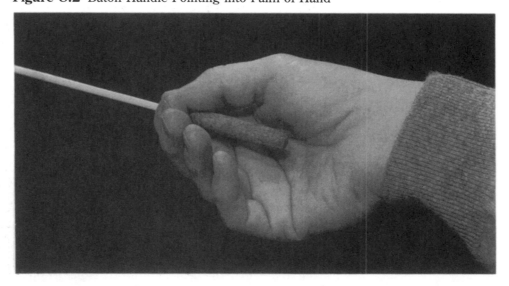

Figure 8.3
Baton Tip on Vertical Plane

Figure 8.4 *Marcato* Grip for Baton

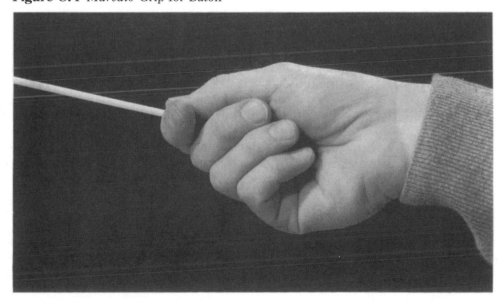

Figure 8.5
Incorrect Double Plane
(Hand and Baton)

Another problem is insufficient breadth on a beat that moves to the right, with the tip of the baton stopping at a point inward from the hand. This problem is caused by a stiff elbow and a forearm that fails to extend enough to the right. Remember that the ictus is defined by the point of the baton, and the point must move to the perimeter of the conducting area.

If the wrist tends to be floppy, use of the baton will only magnify this motion, and a rigid wrist will look more rigid with a baton. The wrist should be flexible, which translates to a clear ictus with the baton.

Finally, use of the baton may exaggerate the rebound movement, causing the ictus to be obscured. The rule remains the same when using a baton: The height of the rebound should be no more than half that used for the amplitude of the vertical plane.

When used correctly, the baton will extend naturally, and the tip of the baton will define the ictus. The vertical plane is now transferred from the right of the body to the center, as in Figure 8.3.

GUIDED PRACTICE

1. Practice holding the baton correctly while your instructor inspects each student's grip.

2. Practice making downstrokes with the baton while keeping the tip on the new *center* vertical plane.

3. Practice the two, three, and four patterns with the baton. Monitor for proper placement of each ictus on the horizontal plane. Add the preparatory gesture.

4. Practice varying the size of the pattern with the baton. Return to the dynamic-change exercises in Examples 7.1 and 7.2, and conduct those with the baton.

5. Practice Daily Dozens with the baton.

6. Practice *Chester, Austrian Hymn, My Country, 'Tis of Thee,* and "Ode to Joy" with the baton.

CHARACTER TERMINOLOGY

Many different words are used by composers to describe the appropriate character of music. As with tempo and dynamics terms, these are often in Italian. A listing of all words that may be encountered is impossible, and all conductors should have music and language dictionaries available as they study scores. Some of the most frequently used terms are listed here.

Italian	English
Dolce	Sweetly
Sotto voce	Subdued voice
Con brio	With vigor
Animato	Animated
Giocoso	Humorously
Espressivo	Expressively
Tranquillo	Gently
Cantabile	Singing
Dolente	Sad, mournful
Grave	Solemn
Con fuoco	With fire
Vivace	Lively
Pesante	Heavy
Maestoso	Majestic
Scherzando	Playful, jesting
Semplice	Simple, unaffected
Agitato	Agitated
Con bravura	With boldness
A capriccio	Whimsical
Con tenerezza	With tenderness

ASSIGNMENT

1. Study Character Terminology for a quiz in the next class session.
2. Practice all conducting gestures with the baton. Monitor for a correct grip and placement of each ictus on the horizontal plane. Use a full-length mirror.
3. Practice the Daily Dozens with the use of a baton.
4. Practice *My Country, 'Tis of Thee* (in three) and "Ode to Joy" (in two) with the baton for individual presentation in the next class session (Videotaping #2).

■ Videotaping #2

This is your second time for individual conducting before the class, now using the baton. Some nervousness is still to be expected; remain calm and trust yourself.

Objectives for this second videotaping are

- proper posture and arm/hand positioning
- preparatory set and correct preparatory gesture
- eye contact and rhythmic breathing motion
- clear three and two patterns with internal and final releases
- correct use of the baton
- communication of musical affect

Preparation

Many of the techniques you are learning are just beginning to become habitual, but you have learned much about conducting in these first eight lessons. If you have practiced faithfully each day, your confidence will begin to show. **Remember: Do not advertise your mistakes!**

Read the elements that will be evaluated in this second videotaping as found on Evaluation Form II in this lesson, which will serve as a good review of all gestures and techniques studied thus far. Notice the new section on baton grip and use. As before, view the videotape of your conducting and follow the directives as to the use of the form. The instructor will make constructive comments on the tape, which will help you to complete the self-evaluation form.

When you are called upon to conduct, proceed to the conductor's stand, place your music on it, and fix the tempo in your mind *before* raising your head and arm. Once you are set to begin, raise your head and arm simultaneously, scan the group with your eyes, give the preparatory gesture with rhythmic breathing motion and keep your eyes up on the downbeat. The two musical examples will be conducted by each student in succession: *My Country, 'Tis of Thee* (in three), and "Ode to Joy" (in two).

If something goes wrong with your conducting at the very beginning, stop and begin again (call a "let" ball); initial nervousness will sometimes cause a bad start.

If, however, you lose your place or the pattern falters during the music—keep going! You must find a way to the end if only by giving a series of downbeats.

Lastly, try to communicate each musical example. Ask yourself, "what do I want to communicate to the audience in this piece of music?" No matter how good your technique is, you will be unconvincing if you do not convey the meaning and mood of each piece.

When it is someone else's turn to conduct, be a good ensemble member. Respond to the person conducting, sing or play out, and follow the tempo given. Hold your music up and maintain eye contact. Do not practice your conducting while seated; this confuses the conductor and shows that you are not actively participating as an ensemble member.

GUIDED PRACTICE

1. Warm up by group practice of *My Country, 'Tis of Thee* (in three) and "Ode to Joy" (in two).

2. Now is the time to ask any last-minute questions.

VIDEOTAPING #2—*MY COUNTRY, 'TIS OF THEE* (Anonymous) AND "ODE TO JOY" (Beethoven)

ASSIGNMENT

1. View Videotaping #2 in the location designated by your instructor. Complete Evaluation Form II on both sides, and turn it in to the instructor as requested.

2. Continue the practice of the Daily Dozens with the baton.

3. Read Lesson 10 in preparation for the next class session.

Name _____   Date ____ / ____ / ____

EVALUATION FORM II

Complete the self-evaluation below. Leave those elements blank that are basically correct; use + for very good elements and − for those that need improving.

Posture—Arm/Hand Positioning

_____ proper foot position	_____ upper arm forward
_____ knees relaxed	_____ elbow lifted
_____ straight spine	_____ forearm—upper arm angle
_____ sternum up	_____ forearm extended
_____ shoulders back/down	_____ proper hand position
_____ head high	_____ fingers naturally curved

Preparation

_____ mental set	_____ correct tempo
_____ group scan	_____ correct dynamic level
_____ smooth preparatory gesture	_____ correct articulation
_____ rhythmic breathing motion	_____ clear ictus
_____ eye contact	_____ confident and assuring demeanor

Four Pattern and Releases

_____ vertical plane location	_____ pattern clarity
_____ vertical plane amplitude	_____ internal releases
_____ horizontal plane location	_____ final release
_____ horizontal breadth	_____ release preparation
_____ clear ictus on each beat	_____ communication

Baton Grip and Use

_____ proper contact points	_____ baton on vertical plane
_____ natural curve of fingers	_____ ictus at baton tip
_____ correct direction of baton	_____ ictus on horizontal plane

Evaluation Summary. Summarize your conducting evaluation in narrative form. Write one paragraph summarizing the positive elements of your conducting and one paragraph on those elements that need improving.

Summarize positive elements:

Summarize those elements in need of improvement:

Lesson 10

■ The One Pattern
■ Midterm Preparation
■ Release on One
■ Accent, Articulation, and Connecting Terms

Continue to monitor your use of the baton; little technical problems can creep into one's handling of the baton very quickly and all too often end up being big problems.

Objectives for this lesson are
• executing the one pattern
• a new release on count one
• continuing to refine baton use
• applying techniques to musical examples
• accent, articulation, and connecting terminology

GUIDED PRACTICE

1. Review the characteristics of the baton grip and positioning. Monitor yourself and classmates for any problems detected in Videotaping #2.

2. Elect several students to lead the class in unison Daily Dozens with the baton.

THE ONE PATTERN

The one pattern is used to conduct one pulse per measure; this occurs most often in duple or triple meter when the tempo is too fast to conduct the individual beats. The pulse may feel like only one beat, or a subtle feeling of division may be felt/executed on the upward motion of the pattern, depending upon the metric and melodic accents of the music.

The diagram of the one pattern with no feeling of division is shown in Figure 10.1. This simple down-up motion denotes but one ictus; the upward rebound is quick and does not show a divided beat. This type of gesture might be used for music that is strongly accented.

Music that is *legato* needs a gesture that is more rounded, like that in Figure 10.2.

Figure 10.1 One Pattern with Quick Rebound

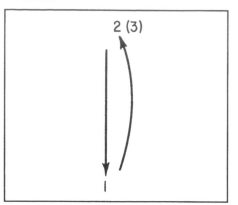

Figure 10.2 One Pattern (*Legato*)

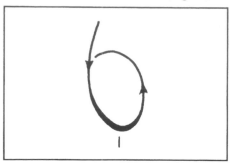

As for all *legato* articulation, the size of the loop or rebound dictates the amount of flow or smoothness; the greater the oval shape the more *legato* the articulation. The movement of the gesture is down and forward from the body at a forty-five-degree angle, with the motion moving counterclockwise–down and out, not sideways, and not straightforward.

Some types of music (especially quick waltzes, in triple meter) have a strong feeling of division, even though the music moves basically in one. The rebound following the downbeat is then divided either by light pulses of the wrist/hand on beats two and three, or by stopping (ever so briefly) halfway up the rebound for beat two, and continuing upward with a lift of the hand/baton on beat three.

GUIDED PRACTICE

1. Practice the one patterns diagrammed in Figures 10.1 and 10.2.

2. Practice dividing the pulse of the one pattern in triple meter. Use *legato* articulation as for a waltz. Monitor for a slight pulsing action on beats two and three.

3. Practice the theme to the *Emperor Waltz* by Johann Strauss (Example 10.1). As for some waltzes, the meter is triple, but the feeling is in one. As this example is *legato,* use the conducting pattern for one as given in Figure 10.2.

4. The "Waltz" from the ballet *Coppélia* by Léo Delibes (Example 10.2) is an example of conducting in one with a divided gesture. The beat on one rebounds and stops midway up the vertical plane on two, followed by a quick upward motion on beat three. This stop-start motion on the rising rebound is especially important when the melodic phrase begins each time on a pickup beat (beat three). While there is a strong feeling of triple meter, the tempo moves quickly, and the gesture is awkward when conducted in three. Therefore, conduct this excerpt in a divided one, but keep the gesture smooth (rounded), minimizing the stop-start action from beat two to beat three.

Example 10.1 Theme from *Emperor Waltz*

J. Strauss

Example 10.2 "Waltz" Theme from *Coppélia*

L. Delibes

MIDTERM PREPARATION

Sing We and Chant It by Thomas Morley

Sing We and Chant It (Example 10.3) is an English Renaissance ballet (madrigal). While it is in triple meter, its infectious spirit demands that this composition be conducted in a straight and springing "one." It is the first of four compositions to be conducted on the midterm conducting exam.

An internal cutoff occurs in measure eight, before the *piano* repeat. To execute this gesture, measure eight must be subdivided: beat one rebounds and stops halfway up the vertical plane for beat two; the gesture then continues upward for beat three, upon which the ensemble breathes. This happens very quickly. Beat three (quarter rest) is actually the preparation gesture for the repeat, and a smaller, upward gesture must be used to indicate the *piano* dynamic level. After the first eight measures are repeated, the preparatory gesture in measure eight must of necessity be larger, to anticipate the *forte* dynamic level in measure nine.

The second part of *Sing We and Chant It* (measures 9–23) is a good example of *subito* dynamic changes. It begins with four measures of *forte,* followed by four measures of *piano.* Two measures of *forte* (17–18) change quickly to *piano* (measure 19) in the lower vocal parts. Remember from Lesson 9 that sudden dynamic changes must be prepared on the beat *prior* to the beat on which the dynamic change occurs. Therefore, the measure before each dynamic change must be subdivided in order that the third beat may be shown smaller (when changing to *piano*) or larger (when changing to *forte*).

The preparatory gesture for *Sing We and Chant It* is the same as that used for the other common patterns: it begins to the right of the vertical plane, moves downward to the horizontal plane for the preparatory ictus, rebounds, and moves downward on the downbeat. Notice that the preparatory gesture moves with a clockwise motion, while the flow of the one pattern is counterclockwise. This can be confusing to beginning conducting students.

RELEASE ON ONE

The final release previously learned occurs on the last beat of the final measure. It may be more musically satisfying if the music continues for the duration of the entire measure, ending on the downbeat following the last measure. This is sometimes called the "downstroke" release.

Sing We and Chant It requires a downstroke cutoff as a final release; to release on beat three of the last measure would be too abrupt. Therefore, the conductor releases on the downbeat following the double bar.

To execute the downstroke cutoff, the rebound before the downstroke is exaggerated by elevating the arm/hand/baton higher, with a slight lifting of the chin/head. There is a slight pause at the top of the rebound, followed by the simultaneous dropping of the chin/head and arm/hand/baton on the downbeat following the double bar. The downward movement of the chin/head and arm/hand/baton must stop together at the moment of release with no rebound. Because there is no circular motion in the preparation for this cutoff, the lifting and lowering of the chin/head, as well as the exaggeration of the rebound gesture, both serve to signal the ensemble that the cutoff is about to occur. The final downstroke cutoff for *Sing We and Chant It* is diagrammed in Figure 10.3.

Example 10.3 *Sing We and Chant It*   Conduct in 1   **T. Morley**

Example 10.3a Instrumental Parts for *Sing We and Chant It*

Figure 10.3 Downstroke Release

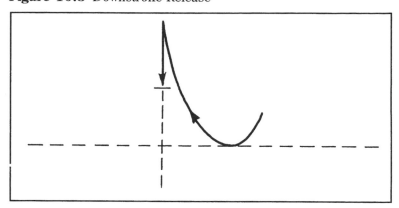

GUIDED PRACTICE

1. Observe the instructor modeling *Sing We and Chant It*, immediately follow this model with group practice in unison. The repeat at measure eight should be taken, but because of time limitations, the repeat of the second part of the composition has been omiited.

2. Special practice will be needed for the internal cutoffs and final release. Watch the instructor model each of these cutoffs, and practice them separately from the music.

Divertimento No. 1 in B-flat, "Andante" (formerly attributed to F. J. Haydn)

The "Chorale St. Antonii" was set by Haydn as a divertimento for winds. It is the second composition of four that will be conducted on the midterm exam. The meter is duple, the tempo is *andante,* the articulation is *legato,* and the dynamic level begins *piano.*

There are two 5-measure phrases in the first part. The first five measures are *piano,* while the second five are *forte.* The rebound of beat two in measure five needs to be larger to indicate the dynamic change to *forte* in measure six.

There is an internal release in measure ten This is the same release on two as used for *Chester* in cut time. However, the rebound of beat two must stop halfway up the vertical plane, and then continue upward with a smaller gesture to prepare the *piano* dynamic level in measure eleven (Figure 10.4).

The dynamic level changes to *pianissimo* in measure fifteen. This must be anticipated with the rebound of the internal cutoff in measure fourteen. The rebound action as it lifts from beat two must be very small to indicate the very soft dynamic level that is to come.

There is a *crescendo-decrescendo* in measures seventeen-eighteen. While such a dynamic change might more easily be shown by the left hand, the right hand/baton is also capable of communicating this change in dynamics. Notice in Figure 10.5 that beat two rises from the horizontal plane to indicate the quick *crescendo.* The quick *decrescendo* is shown in Figure 10.6, where beat one lowers halfway, and beat two lowers to its normal position on the vertical plane. This "stepping up" and "stepping down" sequence needs to be carefully shaped by the baton so as to be clear to the ensemble.

The internal cutoff in measure eighteen may be shown by a brief stopping action on beat two. The rebound of beat two must be rather large to prepare the *forte* dynamic level in measure nineteen. There is no internal cutoff in measure twenty-two, but the rebound of beat two must be very large to indicate the *fortissimo* dynamic level in measure twenty-three. The *diminuendo* that begins in measure twenty-eight and continues to the end requires a gradual reduction in the size of the two pattern. A downstroke cutoff is used at the end of the composition.

GUIDED PRACTICE

1. As the instructor models "Chorale St. Antonii," sing the melody on a neutral syllable, followed by the class practicing in unison. Practice each section separately.

2. Special practice will be needed for the internal cutoffs, *crescendo-decrescendo,* preparation of sudden dynamic changes, and final release. The instructor should model each of these elements as you practice them separately from the whole

Figure 10.4 Internal Release on Beat Two

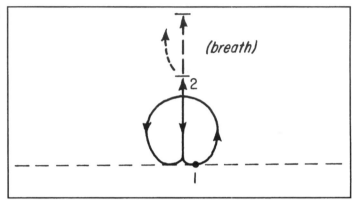

Figure 10.5 Two Pattern: *Crescendo*

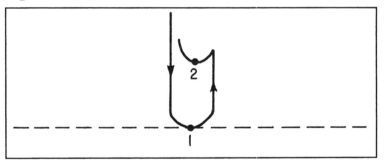

Figure 10.6
Two Pattern: *Decrescendo*

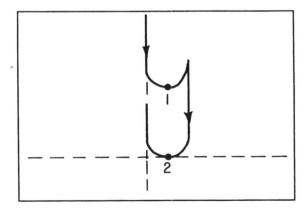

Example 10.4 "Chorale St. Antonii"   **Adapted by F. J. Haydn**

all you peo - ple. Thanks we bring for all life's boun - ties;— thanks we bring for

all life's good - ness.— Now and ev - er - more.

Example 10.4a Instrumental Parts for "Chorale St. Antonii"

C instruments

Bb instruments

C instruments

F instruments

Eb instruments

C instruments

ACCENT, ARTICULATION, AND CONNECTING TERMS

Accent Terms	Definition
Tonic accent	Accent by rise of pitch, rather than by stress
Dynamic accent	Accent by stress or reinforcement
Natural accent	Accent on the downbeat
Secondary accent	Accent on a beat other than the downbeat, e.g., beat three in common time
Irregular accent	Accent on a normally unaccented beat
Agogic accent	Accent by longer duration of a note
Sforzando/Forzando	Accent by forcing/pressure
Rinforzando	Accent by strengthening

Articulation Terms	
Legato	Smoothly connected
Marcato	Marked emphasis
Staccato	Detached
Tenuto	Held, sustained
Portato	Slurred staccato
Staccatissimo (wedge)	Very short and detached; equivalent to the staccato from Couperin to Beethoven

Connecting Terms

Attacca	Two movements should be connected
Attacca subito	with no break, the one following
Segue	immediately after the other.

ASSIGNMENT

1. Study Accent, Articulation, and Connecting Terms for a quiz in the next class session.
2. Continue the practice of Daily Dozens, now adding the one pattern to each set.
3. Practice *Sing We and Chant It* for the midterm conducting exam.
4. Practice "Chorale St. Antonii" for the midterm conducting exam.
5. Read Lesson II in preparation for the next class session.

Lesson 11

- ■ Release on Beat Two
- ■ Entrance on a Pickup Note
- ■ Midterm Preparation

You will study two additional compositions in this lesson in preparation for the midterm conducting exam. These compositions represent a synthesis of the conducting techniques studied in the first half of this method.

Objectives for this lesson are
- ● executing the internal release on beat two
- ● entering on a pickup note
- ● applying conducting technique to musical examples

GUIDED PRACTICE

> 1. Observe as the instructor models the conducting of *Sing We and Chant It,* and practice it in unison. Monitor especially for changes in dynamic levels.
>
> 2. Observe as the instructor models the conducting of "Chorale St. Antonii," and practice it in unison. Monitor especially for changes in dynamic levels.

RELEASE ON BEAT TWO

The internal cutoff on beat two in triple meter is diagrammed in Figure 11.1. Notice that the rebound of beat one circles counterclockwise for the preparation of the cutoff. The release motion extends to the right and upward; this places the baton in position for the inward stroke on beat three.

As with other internal cutoffs, the conducting gesture must stop to indicate the pause. If the tempo is fast, the stop will be simultaneous with the breath. At a slower tempo, the stopping action may be followed immediately by a gentle lift of the baton to indicate the breath (Figure 11.2) before the motion reverses inward to execute beat three.

The internal cutoff on beat two in common time is diagrammed in Figure 11.3. Notice that the rebound of beat one circles counterclockwise to the left of the vertical plane (preparation) and then continues upward on the vertical plane to the cut-

Figure 11.1 Internal Release on Beat Two in Triple Meter

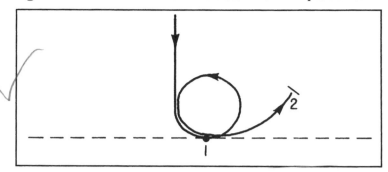

Figure 11.2 Internal Release followed by Breath

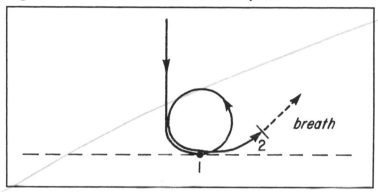

Figure 11.3 Internal Release on Beat Two in Common Time

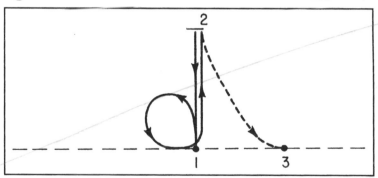

off; this places the baton in position for the movement to beat three, which is down and to the right. Again, if the tempo is fast, the release and breath will be simultaneous at the cutoff. If the tempo is slow, the baton may lift slightly following the cutoff to indicate the breath before proceeding to beat three.

GUIDED PRACTICE

1. Watch the instructor model the internal cutoff on beat two in triple meter, and practice it in unison.

2. Watch the instructor model the internal cutoff on beat two in common time, and practice it in unison.

ENTRANCE ON A PICKUP NOTE

Up to now, all of the musical examples have begun on a downbeat, and the same basic preparatory gesture has been used. Not all music begins on a downbeat, however, and so it is necessary to learn how to execute a preparatory gesture for music that begins on a pickup beat.

The most common type of pickup note is one beat in duration, with no notated rests before it. This will be the last count in the meter, whether in duple, triple, or quadruple time (beat two in duple, beat three in triple, and beat four in quadruple). In each case, the preparatory gesture moves rightward from the vertical plane in a downward and upward gesture that is just the opposite of that used for music beginning on a downbeat (Figure 11.4). This preparatory gesture for a pickup note must finish upward so as to indicate the rhythmic breathing motion. (Preparatory gestures are never given in a downward direction.) The movement then reverses inward to the horizontal plane to execute the pickup ictus (beat two, three, or four).

We have learned how to give preparatory gestures for a downbeat and a pickup beat. Sometimes, however, music begins on a leftward beat (as on beat two in common time), or a rightward beat (as on beat two in triple time or beat three in common time). The preparatory gesture for beginning on beat two in common time is diagrammed in Figure 11.5. Notice that it begins to the left of the vertical plane and moves rightward across the vertical plane and upward for the breath. The motion is then reversed to execute beat two to the left.

The preparatory gesture for beginning on beat two in triple meter or beat three in common time is diagrammed in Figure 11.6. Notice that it begins to the right of the vertical plane and moves leftward across the vertical plane and upward for the

The prep. gestures shews the beat preceding the entrance

Figure 11.4 Preparatory Gesture for a Pickup Note

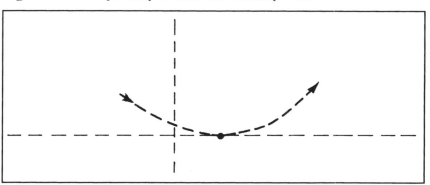

Figure 11.5 Preparatory Gesture for a Leftward Beat

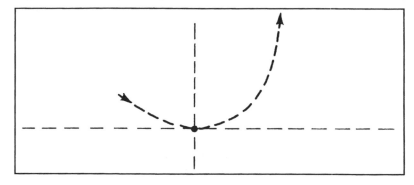

Figure 11.6 Preparatory Gesture for a Rightward Beat

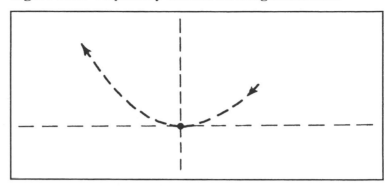

breath. The motion is then reversed to execute beat two (duple meter) or three (quadruple meter). As for all preparatory gestures, preparations from the right or left must move in tempo and communicate the dynamic level and articulation. Also, rhythmic breathing motion is required as well as eye contact.

Example 11.1 Theme A from *Symphony No. 94*, Movement 3   **F. J. Haydn**

Example 11.2 Theme B from *Symphony No. 94*, Movement 3   **F. J. Haydn**

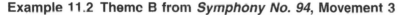

GUIDED PRACTICE

1. Observe the instructor model the preparatory gesture for a pickup beat, and practice in unison.

2. Observe the instructor model the preparatory gestures for entrances on a leftward or rightward beat, and practice in unison.

3. Practice the opening theme from movement three of Haydn's *Symphony No. 94 in G Major* ("Surprise") (Example 11.1). Give a strong preparatory gesture to the right to indicate the *forte* dynamic.

4. Practice the second theme or trio section from movement three of Haydn's *"Surprise" Symphony* (Example 11.2). This theme is marked *piano* in contrast to the first theme, and the preparatory gesture for the pickup beat must reflect this dynamic change.

MIDTERM PREPARATION

Erlaube mir by Johannes Brahms

Johannes Brahms set a number of German folk melodies, of which *Erlaube mir* (Example 11.3) is a beautiful example. The dynamic level is *piano,* and the character is marked "tenderly." Such a mood calls for an extremely *legato* articulation with just a slight ictus. This is the third musical example that will be conducted on the midterm exam.

Notice that the composition is in triple meter and begins with a pickup note, which is beat three. Therefore, a left-to-right preparatory gesture, as in Figure 11.4, is used.

There are internal cutoffs on beat two in measures four and eight. (Ignore the internal cutoff in the soprano and alto parts in measure twelve, as the tenor and bass parts do not have the quarter rest. This internal cutoff for soprano and alto would be executed by the left hand.) Review the internal release in Figure 11.1 for this cutoff on beat two in triple meter. Because the tempo is slow, the cutoff may be followed by a gentle lift (on the "and" of beat two) to indicate the breath, as in Figure 11.2. The gesture then flows inward to execute beat three, the beginning of the next phrase.

A *crescendo-decrescendo* is indicated in measures eleven and twelve. Again, a step-up, step-down motion of the baton will be used to indicate this subtle change in dynamics. The *crescendo* in measure eleven is diagrammed in Figure 11.7. Notice that beat two rises approximately one third the distance above the horizontal plane, while beat three is placed about two thirds above the plane. This stepping-up action conveys the feeling of swell in the music.

The *decrescendo* in measure twelve is diagrammed in Figure 11.8. Notice that beat one lowers only about one third of the way, and beat two lowers two thirds, to approximately the same point where beat two lifted for the *crescendo*. Beat three then returns to its normal position on the horizontal plane. This stepping-down movement conveys the decrease in dynamic level for the *decrescendo.*

The final cutoff in bar sixteen is on beat two. (You learned this release earlier for a final release on two in duple meter.) Remember to keep the tail of the final cutoff parallel to the horizontal plane and to pause at the release before lowering the arm.

GUIDED PRACTICE

> Observe the instructor model each of the elements for conducting *Erlaube mir,* and practice in unison. Those elements that will require special attention are: (1) the preparation for a pickup note; (2) the small and very *legato* gesture needed to convey the style; (3) the internal cutoffs in measures four and eight; (4) the *crescendo-decrescendo* in measures eleven–twelve; and (5) the final release.

Figure 11.7 *Crescendo* in Triple Meter

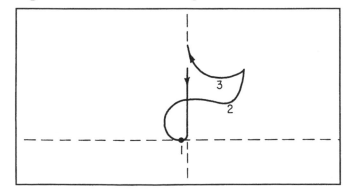

Figure 11.8 *Decrescendo* in Triple Meter

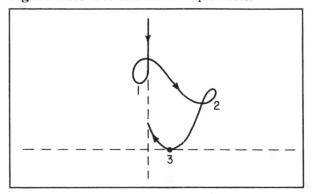

Example 11.3 *Erlaube mir*

Permit me, lovely maiden,
to go into the garden
so that I may see there
how beautiful are the roses.

Permit me to pluck them,
for it is time.
Their beauty has delighted my heart.

Example 11.3a Instrumental Parts for *Erlaube mir*

"Praise Ye the Lord of Hosts" by Camille Saint-Saëns

"Praise Ye the Lord of Hosts" (Example 11.4) is the final movement of the *Christmas Oratorio,* which Saint-Saëns composed for chorus and orchestra. It is a full, majestic piece and requires a very marked ictus.

Internal releases are marked in measures two and four. These are editorial and are placed here for practice purposes. The same gesture is used here as for the cutoff on beat four in *Chester.* No cutoff is marked between measures six and seven, and measures five–eight should be conducted as one phrase. An internal cutoff on beat four does occur in measure eight.

Note the sudden dynamic change to *mezzo forte* in measure nine. This must be prepared by a smaller gesture on the "and" of beat four in measure eight. The baton can be lifted only slightly for the breath and to indicate the forthcoming change. The size of the pattern is then to be reduced for measures nine–twelve.

There is an internal release on beat two in measure twelve. Normally, this would be indicated by the left hand, but because all parts are moving rhythmically the same, the right hand can execute the cutoff. Review the diagram in Figure 11.3 for the movement of this gesture.

A *crescendo* begins in measure thirteen and peaks on the downbeat of measure fifteen. A general expansion of the beat pattern will suffice for indicating this gradual increase in dynamic level.

An internal release occurs on beat one of measure fifteen, before the final "Alleluia." Again, this would be conducted by the left hand, but the right hand also is involved. The gesture for the right hand/baton is a forceful downbeat and a rebound that springs upward. The rebound movement momentarily stops before proceeding left to beat two.

The final release is on beat four in measure sixteen. This is the same type of counterclockwise "C" cutoff used for *Chester.*

Example 11.4 "Praise Ye the Lord of Hosts" from *Christmas Oratorio*   C. Saint-Saëns

earth. Re - joice in the Name of the Lord, for He com - eth, Al - le - lu - ia.

earth. Re - joice in the Name of the Lord, for He com - eth, Al - le - lu - ia.

Example 11.4a Instrumental Parts for "Praise Ye the Lord of Hosts"

GUIDED PRACTICE

1. Observe the instructor model each of the elements for conducting "Praise Ye the Lord of Hosts," and practice in unison. Those elements that will require special attention are: (1) a marked ictus at a *forte* dynamic level; (2) the internal cutoffs in measures two, four, eight, twelve, and fifteen; (3) the sudden dynamic change in measure nine; (4) the *crescendo* in measures twelve–fifteen; and (5) the final release.

2. Review conducting of *Sing We and Chant It* and "Chorale St. Antonii" for individual conducting in the next class session.

ASSIGNMENT

1. Practice *Sing We and Chant It* and "Chorale St. Antonii" for individual presentation and videotaping in the next class session.

2. Review and practice conducting *Erlaube mir* and "Praise Ye the Lord of Hosts." Use a full-length mirror. Consult with the instructor if you are having problems with any of the last four conducting assignments.

■ Videotaping #3

This lesson is the third videotaping session in which you will conduct before the class. Review the procedures from Videotapings #1 and #2. Each student will conduct the two musical selections in succession. View the videotape and complete Evaluation Form III at the end of the lesson.

Objectives for this lesson are

- standard posture and arm/hand position for conducting
- preparatory set and proper preparatory gesture
- eye contact and rhythmic breathing motion
- correct dynamic levels and articulations
- confident use of basic patterns and releases
- proper use of the baton
- communication of musical affect

Preparation

The two selections to be conducted today are the first of the four examples to be conducted on the midterm exam. These four pieces represent a synthesis of the techniques studied in Lessons 1–11. You will want to spend much time practicing these four selections. Although they are rather simple and short, they present a challenge to the beginning conductor. Memorize these four selections and use the music only as a reference.

GUIDED PRACTICE

1. Practice *Sing We and Chant It* and "Chorale St. Antonii" in unison as a warmup.

2. Now is the time to ask your instructor any questions you may have about conducting the above two pieces.

VIDOETAPING #3—*SING WE AND CHANT IT* (Morley) AND "CHORALE ST. ANTONII" (Haydn)

ASSIGNMENT

1. View Videotaping #3, Complete Evaluation Form III on both sides, and turn it in to the instructor.
2. Practice *Erlaube mir* and "Praise Ye the Lord of Hosts" for individual presentation during the next class session (Videotaping #4).
3. Practice *Sing We and Chant It* and "Chorale St. Antonii."

Name _____ Date _____/_____/_____   ┌─────┬─────┐
                                                                          └─────┴─────┘
                                                                            Grades

EVALUATION FORM III

Complete the self-evaluation below. Leave those elements blank that are basically correct; use + for very good elements and − for those that need improving.

Posture—Arm/Hand Positioning

_____ proper foot position   _____ upper arm forward

_____ knees relaxed   _____ elbow lifted

_____ straight spine   _____ forearm—upper arm angle

_____ sternum up   _____ forearm extended

_____ shoulders back/down   _____ proper hand position

_____ head high   _____ fingers naturally curved

Preparation

_____ mental set   _____ correct tempo

_____ group scan   _____ correct dynamic level

_____ smooth preparatory gesture   _____ correct articulation

_____ rhythmic breathing motion   _____ clear ictus

_____ eye contact   _____ confident and assuring demeanor

Patterns and Releases

_____ vertical plane location   _____ pattern clarity

_____ vertical plane amplitude   _____ internal releases

_____ horizontal plane location   _____ final release

_____ horizontal breadth   _____ release preparation

_____ clear ictus on each beat   _____ communication

Baton Grip and Use

_____ proper contact points   _____ baton on vertical plane

_____ natural curve of fingers   _____ ictus at baton tip

_____ correct direction of baton   _____ ictus on horizontal plane

Evaluation Summary. Summarize your conducting evaluation in narrative form. Write one paragraph summarizing the positive elements of your conducting and one paragraph on those elements that need improving.

107

Summarize positive elements:

Summarize those elements in need of improvement:

■ Videotaping #4

This lesson is the fourth videotaping session in which you will conduct before the class. Review the procedures from previous videotapes. Each student will conduct the two musical selections in succession. View the videotape and complete Evaluation Form IV at the end of the lesson.

Objectives for this lesson are
- proper posture and arm/hand positioning
- preparatory set and clear preparatory gestures
- rhythmic breathing motion and eye contact
- correct placement of vertical and horizontal planes
- pattern clarity and internal and final releases
- clear ictus on each beat
- confident use of baton
- dynamic, tempo, and articulation elements
- communication of musical affect

Preparation

The two selections to be conducted in this lesson are the last of the four examples to be conducted on the midterm exam. These four pieces represent a synthesis of the techniques studied in Lessons 1–11. You will want to spend much time practicing these four selections. Although they are rather simple and short, they present a challenge to the beginning conductor. Memorize these four selections and use the music only as a reference.

GUIDED PRACTICE

1. Practice *Erlaube mir* and "Praise Ye the Lord of Hosts" in unison as a warmup.
2. Ask questions and request any final clarifications on the two pieces at this time.

VIDEOTAPING #4—*ERLAUBE MIR* (Brahms) AND "PRAISE YE THE LORD OF HOSTS" (Saint-Saëns)

ASSIGNMENT

1. View Videotaping #4, complete Evaluation Form IV on both sides, and turn it in to the instructor.

2. Practice the four musical examples (Morley, Haydn, Brahms, and Saint-Saëns) for the midterm conducting exam.

Name _____ Date ___/___/___ [|]

EVALUATION FORM IV

Complete the self-evaluation below. Leave those elements blank that are basically correct; use + for very good elements and − for those that need improving.

Posture—Arm/Hand Positioning

_____ proper foot position	_____ upper arm forward
_____ knees relaxed	_____ elbow lifted
_____ straight spine	_____ forearm—upper arm angle
_____ sternum up	_____ forearm extended
_____ shoulders back/down	_____ proper hand position
_____ head high	_____ fingers naturally curved

Preparation

_____ mental set	_____ correct tempo
_____ group scan	_____ correct dynamic level
_____ smooth preparatory gesture	_____ correct articulation
_____ rhythmic breathing motion	_____ clear ictus
_____ eye contact	_____ confident and assuring demeanor

Patterns and Releases

_____ vertical plane location	_____ pattern clarity
_____ vertical plane amplitude	_____ internal releases
_____ horizontal plane location	_____ final release
_____ horizontal breadth	_____ release preparation
_____ clear ictus on each beat	_____ communication

Baton Grip and Use

_____ proper contact points	_____ baton on vertical plane
_____ natural curve of fingers	_____ ictus at baton tip
_____ correct direction of baton	_____ ictus on horizontal plane

Evaluation Summary. Summarize your conducting evaluation in narrative form. Write one paragraph summarizing the positive elements of your conducting and one paragraph on those elements that need improving.

Summarize positive elements:

Summarize those elements in need of improvement:

■ Midterm Conducting Exam, Part 1

This lesson covers the first half of the midterm conducting exam, which requires you to conduct the first pair of selections: *Sing We and Chant It* (Morley) and "Chorale St. Antonii" (Haydn).

Midterm objectives are:
- proper body and arm position
- entrances with eye contact, rhythmic breathing motion, and clear preparatory gesture
- internal and final releases of appropriate size, clear stopping
- beat patterns on the vertical and horizontal planes with adequate horizontal motion, clear ictus, rebound control, appropriate tempo and articulation
- dynamic indications of appropriate size and preparation
- baton use with correct direction and ictus at tip
- musical affect
- confident and assuring presentation

Videotaping Preparation

The exam will be videotaped, but the instructor will make no comments on the tape. Instead, the videotape will be used to view and grade the conducting on the Midterm Conducting Exam form, which is found at the end of this lesson. Each selection to be conducted counts for 25 percent of the midterm grade. Twenty-five elements are graded for each selection. (If an X appears in a box, that element is not graded for that selection.) This form will be returned after the midterm for your own review, evaluation, and comment. As you view the videotape, write an evaluation summary on the back of the form.

All of the techniques learned in Lessons 1–11 can now be demonstrated in polished form. As you prepare for this exam, review all of the elements of posture, arm/hand position, planes, clarity of ictus, patterns, and so on. If you have practiced regularly, these should be automatic gestures about which you must consciously think very little. Your job is to use these gestures to make and communicate music.

GUIDED PRACTICE

1. Warm up using *Sing We and Chant It* and "Chorale St. Antonii."
2. This is the final opportunity to resolve any remaining questions.

MIDTERM CONDUCTING EXAM—PART 1

Sing We and Chant It (Morley)
"Chorale St. Antonii" (Haydn)

ASSIGNMENT

1. Practice *Erlaube mir* and "Praise Ye the Lord of Hosts" for the second part of the midterm conducting exam.
2. Review all of the elements in preparation for Part 2 of the exam.

Name _____ Date ___/___/___

MIDTERM EXAM EVALUATION FORM

Conducting Selections   Points (25 max. each)
1. *Sing We and Chant It*—Morley   _____
2. "Chorale St. Antonii"—Haydn   _____   TOTAL = _____
3. *Erlaube mir*—Brahms   _____
4. "Praise Ye the Lord of Hosts"—Saint-Saëns   _____   GRADE = _____

SUMMARY EVALUATION

No mark indicates **correct**; "−" indicates **incorrect**

	1	2	3	4	REMARKS
POSTURE					
Body position					
Arm position					
ENTRANCES					
Eye contact					
Rhythmic breathing motion					
Clear preparatory gesture					
RELEASES					
Appropriate size					
Clear stop					
Internal					
Final					
BEAT PATTERNS					
Vertical planc					
Horizontal plane					
Horizontal motion					
Clear ictus					
Rebound control					
Appropriate tempo					
Appropriate articulation					
DYNAMIC INDICATIONS					
Appropriate size					
Correct preparation.	(2)				
Subito dynamics			X		
Cresc./decresc.	X		(2)		
BATON USE					
Grip/fingers					
Direction of baton					
Ictus at tip					
MUSICAL AFFECT					
CONFIDENT/ASSURING					
DEMEANOR					

Note: (2) denotes the element is worth two points.

View the video and summarize the strengths of your conducting:

Summarize the weaknesses in your conducting and the areas in which you need to improve:

■ Midterm Conducting Exam, Part 2

This lesson covers the second half of the midterm conducting exam, which requires you to conduct the second pair of selections: *Erlaube mir* (Brahms) and "Praise Ye the Lord of Hosts" (Saint-Saëns).

Midterm objectives are
- proper body and arm position
- entrances with eye contact, rhythmic breathing motion, and clear preparatory gesture
- internal and final releases of appropriate size, clear stopping
- beat patterns on the vertical and horizontal planes with adequate horizontal motion, clear ictus, rebound control, appropriate tempo and articulation
- dynamic indications of appropriate size and preparation
- baton use with correct direction and ictus at tip
- musical affect
- confident and assuring presentation

Videotaping Preparation

The exam will be videotaped, but the instructor will make no comments on the tape. Instead, the videotape will be used to view and grade the conducting on the Midterm Conducting Exam form, the same form that was used for Part 1 of this exam. Each selection to be conducted counts for 25 percent of the midterm grade. Twenty-five elements are graded for each selection. (If an X appears in a box, that element is not graded for that selection.) This form will be returned after the midterm, and you are to view the videotape and write an evaluation summary on the back of the form.

All of the techniques learned in Lessons 1–11 can now be demonstrated in polished form. As you prepare for this exam, review all of the elements of posture, arm/hand position, planes, clarity of ictus, patterns, and so on. If you have practiced regularly, these should be automatic gestures about which you must consciously think very little. Your job is to use these gestures to make and communicate music.

GUIDED PRACTICE

1. Warmup using *Erlaube mir* and "Praise Ye the Lord of Hosts."
2. This is the final opportunity to resolve any remaining questions.

MIDTERM CONDUCTING EXAM—PART 2

Erlaube mir (Brahms)
"Praise Ye the Lord of Hosts" (Saint-Saëns)

ASSIGNMENT

1. When the Midterm Conducting Exam form is returned to you, view the videotapes for Parts 1 and 2, and write a two-paragraph summary (strengths and weaknesses) of your conducting on the back of the form. Did it go as well as you expected? Did you feel comfortable in front of the group? Did nerves get in the way? Express any concerns you may have at this point in the course.

2. Read Lesson 16 in preparation for the next class session.

■ Functions of the Left Hand
■ The Circle Drill

The techniques in the second half of this method build upon those covered in the first half. It is important that you continue to practice daily what was learned previously, as well as the new techniques.

Objectives for this lesson are
- left hand mirroring
- left hand dynamic indications
- four left hand positions
- execution of the Circle Drill

Once you receive the midterm conducting evaluation, make special note of those areas in which you need to concentrate your practice. By now, the basic conducting patterns should be correct and habitual. If not, there will be increasing difficulty as the left hand is used. You cannot forget about the right arm/hand as work now concentrates upon the left arm/hand; continue to review and practice all of the elements learned in the first half of this course. If you have a problem that you cannot seem to correct, make an appointment with the instructor for help.

FUNCTIONS OF THE LEFT HAND

Mirroring

There are many functions of the left hand, the ~~most common~~ *least necessary* of which is *mirroring* the right hand. In mirroring, the left hand does exactly what the right hand does, but the left- and rightward motions are reversed (Figure 16.1). The left hand does not use a baton, therefore the vertical plane is directly in front of the left shoulder. The horizontal plane is identical to that used for the right hand.

All elements of the right arm are the same for the left arm: the elbow is out to the side, the upper arm is extended slightly forward, and the forearm is forward and at an angle slightly more than ninety degrees. The position of the left hand is the same as that learned for the right hand.

The preparatory gesture for the left hand begins to the left of the vertical plane and moves inward, just the opposite of that for the right hand. Both hands move together, and simultaneous downbeats are given.

Figure 16.1 Mirroring Gestures

a. Beat One (Common Time)

b. Beat Two (Common Time)

c. Beat Three (Common Time)

The placement of the beats on the horizontal plane is identical to that used for the right hand, with beats two and three being in the opposite direction of those for the right hand, as Figure 16.1 shows. When conducting in common time with both hands in a mirrored fashion, the inward second-beat motion is somewhat restricted in that the hands are coming toward each other. **The hands must never cross.** When conducting without a baton, the hands will almost touch in the middle on beat two. If using a baton, the right hand should be slightly forward and above so that the baton passes over and in front of the left hand.

One of the biggest problems of conductors is that they mirror with the left hand almost everything the right hand conducts. This is not good technique. Mirroring should be reserved for times when special attention needs to be called to what is happening musically—a *ritardando,* for example, on an *accelerando,* or expressive phrasing. However, it may be necessary to mirror when the ensemble is so large and spread out that members of the group on the left side may not be able to see the pattern clearly without the additional gestures of the left hand. For most conducting, mirroring is not continuously needed, and should be avoided.

There are times when a conductor may wish to transfer the conducting pattern from the right hand to the left, with the right becoming still for those measures or beats. This might occur when something musically is happening exclusively on the left side of the ensemble and needs special attention. Passing the pattern between the hands, while one hand remains still, is a type of mirroring technique.

GUIDED PRACTICE

1. Extend the left arm and hand in a similar position as that learned for the right arm and hand. Monitor for a vertical plane directly in front of the left shoulder. Make vertical strokes on the vertical plane.

2. Practice each of the common patterns (one, two, three, four) with the left hand alone. Place the beats correctly on the horizontal plane. Use a correct preparatory gesture and breathing motion.

3. Practice Daily Dozens while mirroring with left and right hands. Practice first without the baton, then add the baton. Make sure that the hands do not cross on the inward beat. Monitor for an outward beat that extends as fully on the left with the left hand as on the right with the right hand.

4. Practice *Chester* in common time, while mirroring all gestures with both hands. Notice that internal and final releases move in opposite directions when using both hands.

5. Practice the alternating of hands/patterns in Example 16.1. The hand that is conducting moves forward into the conducting area, while the hand that is still draws slightly back toward the body.

Example 16.1 Alternating Right and Left Hands: "Turkish March" Theme from *The Ruin of Athens*
L. van Beethoven

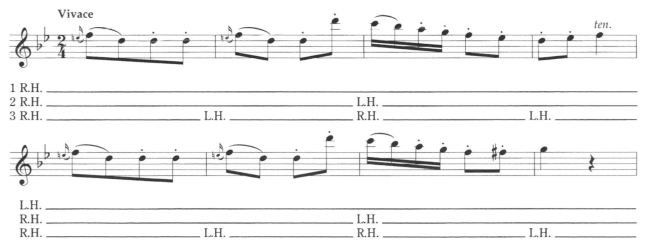

Indicating Dynamic Levels

One of the best uses of the left hand is to indicate dynamic levels. There are basically four types of gestures for this function: (1) palm downward for dynamics indicating soft; (2) palm upward for dynamics indicating loud; (3) palm upward and rising to indicate a *crescendo*; (4) palm downward and lowering to indicate a *decrescendo*; and (5) a "hot touch" or palm outward (briefly) to indicate a slight lowering of the dynamic level.

Left hand dynamic gestures are given with a hand that is a natural extension of the arm. The fingers are naturally curved, and should not stick straight out. Sometimes the hand may be opened more for louder dynamic levels and closed more for softer passages.

The elbow is lowered to the side to execute dynamics with the left arm/hand. To keep it up positions the left hand dynamic gestures inward, rather than straight forward. This is one of the rare times when the elbow may be lowered to properly execute a gesture.

A left palm that faces downward and is lowered to the horizontal plane (parallel to the floor) is an indication of *pianissimo,* or a very soft dynamic level (Figure 16.2). In extremely soft or hushed passages, conductors may push the gesture even lower than the horizontal plane. One must be careful not to place any gesture so low that it cannot be seen easily by the ensemble.

A dynamic level of *piano* is executed with a left palm that faces downward and a left arm that is raised approximately forty-five degrees from the horizontal plane (Figure 16.3). The ensemble members should be able to see into the palm of the partially elevated hand.

Mezzo piano, or moderately soft, is executed by a palm that is more open and an arm that is almost vertical (Figure 16.4). One must be careful not to raise the hand above the shoulder, but to keep it as low as possible while the arm is raised. This will give the message of a dynamic level that is still soft.

A left palm that faces upward and is lowered to the horizontal plane (parallel to the floor) is an indication of *mezzo forte,* or a moderately loud dynamic level (Figure

Figure 16.2 Left Hand Indicating *Pianissimo*

Figure 16.3 Left Hand Indicating *Piano*

16.5). The elbow must be drawn in more toward the body for the *forte* dynamic levels, as this helps to turn the hand upward.

A dynamic level of *forte* is executed with a left palm that faces upward and a left arm that is raised approximately forty-five degrees from the horizontal plane (Figure 16.6). Again, the elbow must be in sufficiently to permit the palm of the hand to be upward.

Figure 16.4 Left Hand Indicating *Mezzo piano*

Figure 16.5 Left Hand Indicating *Mezzo forte*

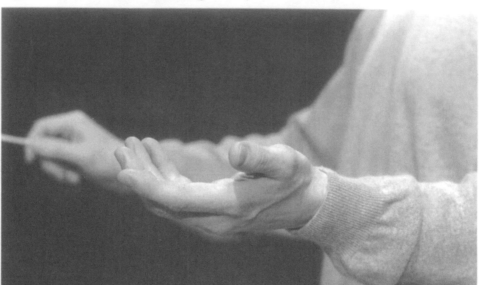

Fortissimo, or very loud, is executed by a palm that is upward and an arm that is extended forward and upward; the hand is at about eye level (Figure 16.7). For louder dynamic levels, the arm/hand is raised even higher, but care should be taken not to raise the left hand over the head. This can be distracting to the audience and should be reserved for very dramatic passages.

When indicating dynamic levels with the left hand, remember that the size of the pattern on the right side must also change to be in agreement with the specified dynamics of the music. The left hand dynamic gesture clarifies and emphasizes that of the right.

Figure 16.6 Left Hand Indicating *Forte*

Figure 16.7 Left Hand Indicating *Fortissimo*

GUIDED PRACTICE

1. Practice the three levels of the left hand gestures for the soft dynamic levels. Conduct patterns with the right hand while indicating the dynamic levels with both hands.

2. Practice the three levels of the left hand gestures for the loud dynamic levels. Conduct patterns with the right hand while indicating the dynamic levels with both hands.

Showing *Crescendo* and *Decrescendo*

A *crescendo* and *decrescendo* are much more clearly shown with the left hand than with the right. Begin the *crescendo* with the left hand on the horizontal plane, palm facing upward. For the *crescendo* gesture, raise the arm/hand in a forward and upward movement to approximately cyc level (Figure 16.8). Keep the arm slightly bent at the peak of the gesture; never extend the arm fully. The hand should be a natural extension of the arm and should not bend at the wrist. Be certain to keep the palm facing upward for the *crescendo*. Keeping the elbow tucked in will help this movement.

When a *crescendo* is to be executed over many measures, it is difficult not to arrive at the peak too soon. This can be remedied by raising the left arm/hand for the first part of the *crescendo,* stopping the gesture at midpoint while the right hand/baton enlarges the pattern, then raising the left hand again to complete the *crescendo* gesture.

The *decrescendo* begins with the palm facing downward, with the hand elevated to approximately eye level and the arm extended forward. Execute the *decrescendo* gesture by gradually lowering and pulling back the left hand to the horizontal plane (Figure 16.9). The rate of lowering the arm will depend on the amount of time/music the *decrescendo* covers.

Figure 16.8 Left Hand Indicating *Crescendo*

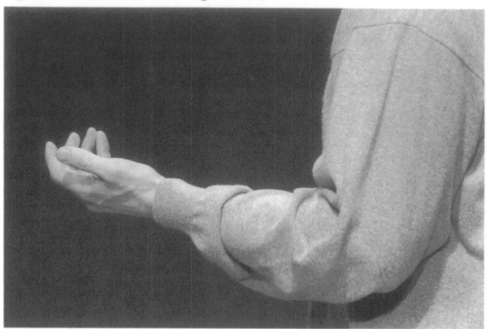

a. Beginning

b. Peak

GUIDED PRACTICE

1. Practice the gestures for the *crescendo* and *decrescendo* following the instructor's model.

2. Practice a *crescendo-decrescendo* gesture in the following manner: (1) hold the left palm upward and outward on the horizontal plane for four counts;

Figure 16.9 Left Hand Indicating *Decrescendo*

a. Beginning

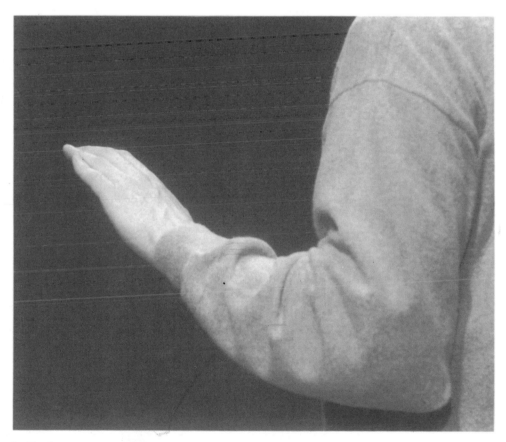

b. End

(2) raise the arm/hand on four counts as for a *crescendo*; (3) hold the peak of the *crescendo* four counts; (4) turn the hand over on the "and" of beat four, and lower it four counts for the *decrescendo*; (5) hold in the *piano* position two counts and turn the hand over (palm up) on the "and" of beat two, hold for beats three and four, and begin the *crescendo* and *decrescendo* pattern again. Practice at first with only the left hand, then add the right arm/hand/baton.

3. Practice a longer *crescendo* with both hands. Raise the left hand four counts (right hand conducting pattern) and stop at midpoint while the right hand/baton enlarges the four pattern. Continue to raise the left hand four counts (right hand continues to conduct pattern) to the peak of the *crescendo*.

4. Conduct the theme of "Ase's Death" from *Peer Gynt*, Op. 46, No. 2, by Edvard Grieg (Example 16.2). Remember to indicate the various dynamic levels with both left and right gestures. The first four measures are *piano*, followed by four measures of *pianissimo*. The *crescendo* in measure nine begins again in measure ten with a sudden drop back to *mezzo-forte*. The *crescendo* in measures fourteen–sixteen must be very controlled so as not to arrive at the peak too soon. The *decrescendo* in measure sixteen is rather a fast decay. The *crescendo* in the first ending increases the dynamic level to *fortissimo* for the repeat. However, hold something back in the size of the gesture for the final *crescendo* in the second ending. Conduct this example in four-bar phrases, with an internal cutoff with the baton at the end of each phrase.

The "Hot Touch"

[handwritten annotation: Lukewarm Touch]

Sometimes a dynamic indication appears in music that requires the sound level to decrease, but not greatly. This is indicated by raising the left hand as in a "stop" gesture (Figure 16.10) for only one beat. It tells the ensemble to decrease the dynamic level only slightly. To keep the hand in this position for too long may indicate too much of a sound level decrease. The left hand must coordinate with the pattern in the right hand to arrive exactly on the beat in which the dynamic change is to occur, and it must be withdrawn quickly in a "hot touch," like a hand from a hot stove.

Example 16.2 "Ase's Death" from *Peer Gynt*, Op. 46, No. 2   **E. Grieg**

Figure 16.10 Left Hand Indicating "Hot Touch"

GUIDED PRACTICE

Practice the "hot touch" gesture by conducting a four pattern with the right hand/baton, showing the hot touch of the left hand on different beats of consecutive patterns. Do not maintain the left hand position for more than one beat.

Four Left Hand Positions

The left hand can be carried or used in four different positions: (1) resting down at the side when only the right hand is needed; (2) resting a little above the waist (close to the body) when it is not being used but will be used shortly; (3) extending into the conducting area to indicate "attention," to mirror, or to show dynamic levels; and (4) extending beyond the normal conducting area for cues (Figure 16.11). You will study the latter position later when learning to cue.

GUIDED PRACTICE

Practice each of the four left hand positions as your instructor models them.

Figure 16.11 Four Positions of Left Hand

a. Resting at Side

b. Resting at Waist

c. Extended for Attention or Mirroring

d. Further Extended for Cueing

THE CIRCLE DRILL

Independence of left and right hands is sometimes difficult to achieve. Students often want to use the left hand to mirror everything they conduct. If the right hand is conducting the patterns automatically, left hand independence will be easier to achieve at this point.

The Circle Drill (Figure 16.12) is an exercise designed to help achieve hand independence. Raise the left arm/hand, as in a "stop" gesture, with the left hand pointing up to 12 on an imaginary clock. Move the left hand in clockwise fashion, pulsing at each hour (1, 2, 3, etc.) on the clock for each beat. Continue around the clock back to 12, and reverse the motion counterclockwise (11, 10, 9, etc.). This is comparable to six measures of music in common time (twenty-four beats). The flow of this left hand motion should be as smooth as possible.

Combine the left hand circle motion with the right hand/baton conducting of the four pattern. Begin slowly and concentrate on keeping the left circle motion moving one "hour" per beat. If the right pattern is automatic, most of the attention can be placed on the left arm/hand. Pulse each of the hours, one per beat. As this becomes easier, the flow of the circle should become smoother and the tempo increased. Practice this exercise daily to gain left hand independence.

Figure 16.12 Left Hand Circle Drill

a. 12:00

Figure 16.12 (*continued*)

b. 3:00

c. 6:00

d. 9:00

GUIDED PRACTICE

1. Practice the left hand Circle Drill as your instructor models it.
2. Practice the Circle Drill with the left hand while the right hand conducts the four pattern. Begin slowly and gradually increase the tempo.

ASSIGNMENT

1. Practice the common patterns (one, two, three, four) with the left hand. Practice the Daily Dozen exercise with the left hand only.
2. Practice the common patterns with left and right hands mirroring. Use the baton in the right hand.
3. Review the six basic dynamic-level positions for the left hand. Practice conducting patterns in common time while holding the left hand in each of the dynamic-level positions (*pp, p, mp, mf, f, ff*).
4. Practice the *crescendo* and *decrescendo* exercises as given in Figures 16.8 and 16.9. Also, practice the *crescendo* exercise that extends longer, the *crescendo* gesture alternating between left and right hands.
5. Practice the Circle Drill for hand independence. Begin slowly and gradually increase the tempo.
6. View the video of your midterm conducting exam, and write a two-paragraph summary of strengths and areas in need of improvement.

Lesson 17

■ Left Hand Sustaining Gestures
■ Coordinating the Two Hands

Conducting with the left hand is always a challenge to people who are right handed. For people who are left handed, however, the challenge has been to learn to conduct with the right hand. In either case, daily practice is the only way to become competent in the basic techniques of conducting.

Objectives for Lesson 17 are

- continued development of left hand independence
- left hand sustaining gestures
- applying the left hand to musical examples

GUIDED PRACTICE

1. Review all of the left hand conducting techniques presented in Lesson 16: (1) conducting of patterns; (2) mirroring; (3) alternate hand conducting; (4) dynamic-level indications; (5) *crescendo* and *decrescendo*; (6) hot touch; and (7) the basic positions and uses of the left hand. Practice each gesture in unison.

2. Select conductors to lead the class in the Circle Drill. Begin slowly, and at this stage do not increase the tempo too quickly. Monitor for trouble with hand independence.

LEFT HAND SUSTAINING GESTURES

The left hand is much used for musical phrasing. Two basic gestures will be studied here: the horizontal sweep and the forward sweep. There are many variations of these sustaining gestures.

The Horizontal Sweep

The horizontal sweep is a gesture often used for *legato* phrasing. The left arm is extended in front of the body with the hand open and thumb up (handshake style). The arm/hand sweeps right to left as if pulling through a heavy liquid (Figure 17.1). The gesture may be reversed with a sweeping action from left to center. For very

Figure 17.1
Left Hand Sustaining
Gesture: Side Sweep

a. Middle Position

b. Sweep to Left

c. Extended Sweep to Left

long phrases, the gesture may flow more in front of the body, but care should be taken that hands do not cross. The greater the feeling of resistance in the flow of the gesture, the greater the communication of a sustained *legato*.

The Forward Sweep

The forward sweep is used to indicate continuous phrasing unbroken by a breath. The left arm is extended before the body with hand open and thumb up (Figure 17.2). For this gesture the hand sweeps slowly forward and gives a little push at the point where the phrase is not to be broken with a breath. Care must be taken that the arm/hand not be elevated for this gesture, as ensemble members may confuse this with a *crescendo*. The forward sweep is executed high enough (horizontal plane level) to be seen easily.

GUIDED PRACTICE

1. Practice the horizontal sweep sustaining gesture in unison as you observe the instructor's model.

2. Practice the forward sweep gesture in unison.

3. Conduct the theme from *Finlandia* by Jean Sibelius (Example 17.1), employing the two sustaining gestures. The left hand is to begin at position two ("attention"). The right hand gives the preparatory gesture (left to right as this piece starts on beat two) and conducts the first measure of three beats. On the downbeat of measure two (dotted half note) the left hand sweeps left for a sustained three beats, reverses for beat four, and gives the downbeat on beat one (mirroring), returning to the attention position.

   The forward sweep is used in measure four to indicate the dotted half note tied to the quarter note in measure five. The left hand sweeps forward on beats two–four of measure four and gives a final little push across the bar line to indicate the unbroken phrasing. A slight downstroke cutoff may be given on beat one (measure five) by the left hand to indicate the breath.

The horizontal sweeping gesture is used again in measure six as it was used in measure two. The forward sweeping gesture is used in measure eight to indicate the whole note tied to the quarter. Again, a slight forward push across the bar line is followed by a downstroke cutoff on the downbeat of measure eight. The remaining phrases are conducted the same.

4. Review Lesson 11 and practice the preparatory gesture for beginning on beat two.

Figure 17.2 Left Hand Sustaining Gesture: Forward Sweep

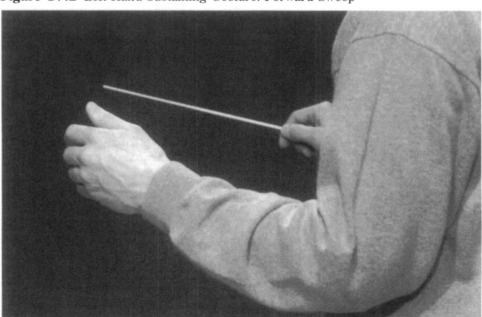

a. Back Position

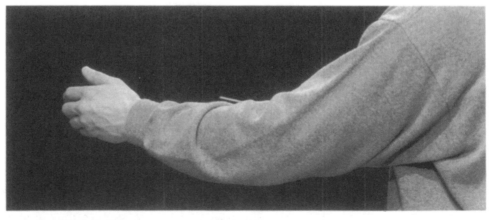

b. Forward Extension

Example 17.1 Theme from *Finlandia* J. Sibelius

COORDINATING THE TWO HANDS

O Beautiful for Spacious Skies by Samuel Ward

Example 17.2, *O Beautiful for Spacious Skies,* requires good left hand/right hand coordination and independence. The right hand/baton begins with a pickup note on beat four; remember that this motion sweeps left to right and upward (breath) for the preparatory gesture. The right hand/baton conducts a straight four pattern for most of the sixteen measures. The right hand pattern, however, must reflect the various dynamic levels.

The left hand gesture at the beginning indicates *mezzo-piano* and remains in this position for the first four measures while the right hand conducts the four pattern. In measure four, the left hand gives only the internal cutoff with a clockwise circle (preparation) on the "and" of beat two, coming to a stop at the left (tail up) for the release on beat three.

The cutoff in measure four does not involve the right hand, which continues to conduct the pattern. Coordinating this left hand release with the four pattern is difficult for beginning conductors but can be mastered by reviewing each movement very slowly. Notice that for the preparation of the cutoff ("and" of beat two), both left and right hands are moving to the right. The left hand, however, moving clockwise, quickly circles down and to the left to beat three, while the right hand/baton continues to the right for beat three. This coordinated action of both hands will become easier if practiced slowly at first, increasing the speed of the motion as it becomes more natural.

The left hand mirrors the right hand on the pickup to and downbeat of measure five. The left hand then returns to indicating the *mezzo piano* dynamic level for measures five and six.

A *crescendo* begins in measure seven and peaks on the downbeat of measure eight. The left hand prepares for this *crescendo* by turning over, palm upward, on the "and" of beat four in measure six. It then begins the *crescendo* movement (forward and upward) on the four beats of measure seven, reaching the peak on the downbeat of measure eight and sustaining with palm upward. The right hand/baton shows the *crescendo* by increasing the size of the pattern to *forte.*

The internal cutoff in measure eight again is given by the left hand only; the palm is facing upward for the *forte* dynamic level. Therefore, as the preparatory gesture begins to circle clockwise on the "and" of beat two, the palm of the left hand turns over facing downward as it moves to the release on beat three. Again, the tail of the cutoff ends upward to indicate the break and breath. The right hand conducts only the pattern.

The third phrase (measures nine–twelve) is conducted *forte* with a *decrescendo* at the end. As before, the left hand mirrors the pickup to and downbeat of measure nine. On the downbeat, the left hand springs open, palm up and arm forward to indicate the *forte* dynamic level. The left hand remains in this position above the horizontal plane, with the baton passing *under* the left arm, not over it.

For each gesture, where something could go wrong,
look at the ensemble!

0

BASIC TECHNIQUES OF CONDUCTING

Example 17.2 *O Beautiful for Spacious Skies*

S. A. Ward

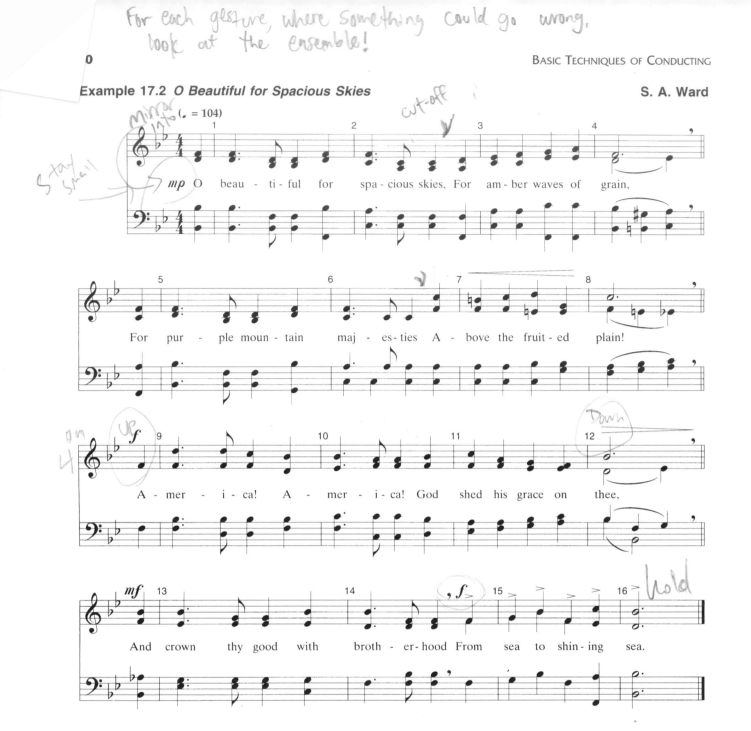

The *decrescendo* in measure twelve is prepared on the "and" of beat four in measure eleven by the left hand turning over and circling clockwise to the palm facing down. The left arm/hand remains high, however, at the *forte* level. The *decrescendo* then begins in measure twelve with a slight lowering of the left hand on beats one and two. The *decrescendo* lowers the hand to the *mezzo-forte* level. The same internal cutoff occurs in measure twelve as in measures four and eight; the left hand begins the preparatory circle, clockwise, on the "and" of beat two and continues to the left, palm down, to beat three for the release. The pattern in the right hand becomes slightly smaller for the *decrescendo*.

The final phrase begins *mezzo forte,* and as before, the left hand mirrors the right hand on the pickup to and downbeat of measure thirteen. The left hand springs open on the downbeat to indicate the *mezzo-forte* level and remains in this gesture until indicating the internal release on beat three in measure fourteen. This is the same type of gesture used in measures four, eight, and twelve.

Example 17.2a Instrumental Part for *O Beautiful for Spacious Skies*

The cutoff in measure fourteen is mirrored by both hands. This is done for dramatic purposes, and because all parts release on beat three. In order for the baton to be positioned correctly for the release, two downbeats (on beats one and two) are given by the right hand/baton in measure fourteen, followed by the preparatory circle (clockwise) on the "and" of beat two. The preparatory circles are mirrored by both hands, with the cutoff gestures going in opposite, outward and upward, directions.

The pickup on beat four of measure fourteen is mirrored by both hands, as are the four beats in measure fifteen. Notice the *marcato* articulation, which requires a decisive and accented gesture.

The final measure is sustained for the full three counts, with the cutoff following the double bar. The left hand sustains (palm up) for beats one, two, and three, while the right hand conducts the pattern. The final release across the double bar is mirrored by both hands. The preparatory circles begin on the "and" of beat three, the left hand moving clockwise, and the right moving counterclockwise. The final release ends with the tails of the cutoff moving outward (in opposite directions) on the horizontal plane.

This arrangement of *O Beautiful for Spacious Skies* is highly edited for teaching purposes. It enables you to use the left hand for a variety of conducting gestures with a relatively simple piece of music.

GUIDED PRACTICE

1. Practice in unison as the instructor models each phrase of *O Beautiful for Spacious Skies* with left hand only.

2. Review the necessary preparatory gesture for a pickup, and practice this gesture with the baton.

3. Observe as the instructor models the internal cutoff for the right hand/baton in measure fourteen (two downbeats), and practice in unison.

> **4.** Practice conducting *O Beautiful* with both hands; take one phrase at a time. The internal release in measures four, eight, twelve, and fourteen will need special attention, although these four cutoffs are identical.

"Break Forth, O Beauteous Heavenly Light" by J. Schop; harm. J. S. Bach

This well-known chorale is from Bach's *Christmas Oratorio* for chorus and orchestra (Example 17.3). (It may be used for supplemental study in this lesson or omitted.) Like the previous example, it begins each new phrase with a pickup of one beat. In the Baroque period (c. 1600–1750), the fermata was used in chorales as a breath mark, rather than an extended hold. The chorales were sung by the congregation during such major works, and frequent pauses were needed. Therefore, each phrase (except the last) ends with one beat, the cutoff for which is the breath for the following phrase. This cutoff/breath should not be rushed; the final beat of each phrase has a feeling of *tenuto* or slight "stretch" in its length.

All of the tempo and dynamic markings are editorial, for the purpose of practice. These markings, however, are in keeping with contemporary performance practice.

As for *O Beautiful,* the left hand alone executes the cutoff at the end of each phrase. Measures one–eight are *forte,* and the left hand may remain in, and return to, a palm-up position following the cutoff at the end of each phrase. The new phrase beginning in measure eight starts *mezzo-piano* and swells to *forte;* use the left hand to indicate these dynamic changes (palm downward to palm upward through the *crescendo*). The final phrase has a *decrescendo* and should be indicated by a palm-downward, slowly descending left hand. The final measure of the chorale should have a slight *ritardando,* which is a common interpretation for most chorales of this period. Using the left hand to mirror in this final measure helps to keep the ensemble together.

GUIDED PRACTICE

> **1.** Conduct with the instructor "Break Forth, O Beauteous Heavenly Light", and practice each phrase first with left hand alone, and then with the addition of the right hand conducting the meter. Remember also that the pattern should change in size according to the dynamic level indicated.
>
> **2.** It is appropriate to mirror the preparation of this example with the left hand, palm up. This preparatory motion for the left hand begins near the center of the body and moves to the left (opposite that of the right hand) before moving inward for the pickup beat. (The left hand mirrors the pickup beat for each new phrase.) It is not appropriate, however, for the left hand to mirror the right hand pattern for each phrase (except for the final measure); use the left hand to indicate the dynamic levels and cutoffs.

ASSIGNMENT

1. Practice the Circle Drill to gain hand independence.
2. Practice the two sustaining gestures, and employ them in conducting Example 17.1 (*Finlandia*). This musical excerpt will be part of the next individual conducting and videotaping before the class.
3. Practice *O Beautiful for Spacious Skies* and/or "Break Forth, O Beauteous Heavenly Light" with left hand alone, right hand alone, and hands together. Analyze each of the measures to understand what each hand is doing at that time. One or both of these compositions will be part of the next individual conducting and videotaping before the class.
4. Read Lesson 18 for the next class session.

Example 17.3 "Break Forth, O Beauteous Heavenly Light"   **by J. Schop, harm. J. S. Bach**

Example 17.3a Instrumental Parts for "Break Forth, O Beauteous Heavenly Light"

Lesson 18

■ Left Hand Strengthening Techniques
■ Repeat Markings

Coordination between hands should be getting better; it is good to practice each hand separately and then together for the musical examples.

Objectives for this lesson are
- strengthening of left hand conducting techniques
- use of repeat markings

LEFT HAND STRENGTHENING TECHNIQUES

GUIDED PRACTICE

1. Choose conductors to lead the class warmup with the Circle Drill. The first conductor leads the drill at a slow tempo, and each successive conductor should increase the tempo. Monitor for those having trouble with this drill.

2. Review briefly all of the left hand conducting techniques presented in Lessons 16 and 17: (1) conducting of patterns; (2) mirroring; (3) alternate hand conducting; (4) dynamic level indications; (5) *crescendo* and *decrescendo*; (6) hot touch; (7) the basic positions and uses of the left hand; and (8) sustaining gestures.

3. Review the excerpt from *Finlandia*, and practice conducting in unison, following the instructor's model.

4. Review *O Beautiful for Spacious Skies* and/or "Break Forth, O Beautiful Heavenly Light" with left hand only and conduct in unison as in the previous example.

5. Review the conducting of *O Beautiful* and/or "Break Forth" with right hand only and conduct in unison.

6. Practice conducting *O Beautiful* and/or "Break Forth" with both hands; take one phrase at a time, and then conduct the whole.

REPEAT MARKINGS

When a phrase or an entire section is repeated, the composer can be spared the work of rewriting the entire section by using various repeat signs. The following are the most common markings used to indicate repetitions.

1. Single Repeat Sign (Example 18.1). A double bar with two dots placed at the end of a phrase or section means "Repeat from the sign back to the beginning."

Example 18.1 Single Repeat Sign

2. Double Repeat Signs (Example 18.2). Two repeat signs facing each other mean "Repeat the music between the two signs."

Example 18.2 Double Repeat Sign

3. First and Second Endings (Example 18.3). A repeat sign is sometimes combined with the first ending, which means "Repeat from the beginning, skip the first ending on the repetition, and proceed to the second ending."

Example 18.3 First and Second Endings

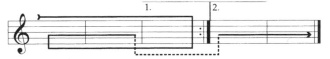

4. *Da capo al fine* (Example 18.4). A repeat sign can be replaced by the Italian term *Da capo* (abbreviated *D.C.*), which means "Repeat from the head" (beginning). If only a portion of the music is to be repeated, the term *fine* ("end") is inserted at the point where the music is to end.

Example 18.4 *Da Capo al Fine*

5. *Dal segno al fine* (Example 18.5). A repeat sign can be replaced by the Italian term *Dal segno,* which means "Repeat from the sign" (not from the beginning). If only a portion of the music is to be repeated, the term *fine* is inserted at the point where the music is to end.

Example 18.5 *Dal Segno al Fine*

6. *Da capo al segno dal fine* (Example 18.6). A first-ending sign can be replaced by the Italian *segno* ("sign"), which means "Repeat from the beginning to the sign, skip the section between the sign and the *D.C.* indication, and proceed from the final section to the end." This is like a first and second ending.

Example 18.6 *Da Capo al Segno dal Fine*

7. *Da capo al segno dal segno* (Example 18.7). First and second endings can be combined with the "circle" sign to indicate a third ending or a codetta. The term means "Repeat from the beginning to the first sign, and continue from the second sign to the end."

Example 18.7 *Da Capo al Segno dal Segno*

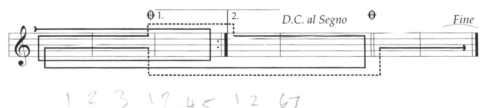

8. 4× (Example 18.8). A number with an × (times) over a number of measures to be repeated means "Repeat the four (or whatever number) measures four (or whatever number) times."

Example 18.8 4× (Repeat the Four Measures Four Times)

9. Vamp (Example 18.9). The term *Vamp*, written above a number of measures to be repeated, means "Continue the repeat at the discretion of the conductor."

Example 18.9 Vamp

10. Double Slash with Dots (Example 18.10). A symbol that is combined with a number above it to indicate the number of previous measures to be repeated. The symbol means "Repeat the previous two (or whatever number) measures." This type of repeat indication is frequently used in show music, jazz, and music of Morton Gould and Leroy Anderson, as well as the 1930s and 1940s editions of Haydn symphonies.

Example 18.10 Double Slash with Dots

ASSIGNMENT

1. Practice the Circle Drill to gain hand independence.
2. Practice the two sustaining gestures, and employ them in conducting Example 17.1 (*Finlandia*). This musical excerpt will be part of the individual conducting and videotaping during the next session.
3. Practice *O Beautiful* and/or "Break Forth" with left hand alone, right hand alone, and hands together. Analyze each measure to understand what each hand is doing at that time. One or both of these compositions will be part of the next individual conducting and videotaping in the next class session.
4. Review Evaluation Form V in Lesson 19.
5. Study Repeat Markings for a quiz on this material in the next class session.

■ Videotaping #5

This is the first videotaping in which you will use the left hand. Some coordination problems are to be expected, but the right hand should be feeling very comfortable by this time.

Objectives for this lesson are
- proper posture and arm/hand positioning
- preparation set and correct preparatory gestures
- clearly communicated patterns using the right arm/hand/baton
- eye contact and rhythmic breathing motion
- coordinated use of the left hand to indicate dynamics, releases, and sustaining gestures

Preparation

Read the elements that will be evaluated in this fifth videotaping as found on "Evaluation Form V" in this lesson. This will serve as a good review of all gestures and techniques studied thus far. Notice that a section on the left hand has been added. Review the videotape of your conducting and follow the directives as to the use of the form. The instructor may make constructive comments on the tape, which will help you to complete the self-evaluation form.

When it is your turn to conduct, proceed to the conductor's stand, place your music on it, and fix the tempo in your mind *before* raising your head and arm. Once you are set to begin, raise your head and arm simultaneously, scan the group with your eyes, give the preparatory gesture with rhythmic breathing motion, and keep your eyes up on the downbeat. Do this for each of the musical examples.

If something goes wrong with your conducting at the very beginning, stop and begin again; even at this stage of experience nervousness will sometimes cause a bad start. If you lose your place, however, or the pattern falters during the music— keep going all the way to the end! The art of successful performance is to continue in the most convincing manner possible, recovering from false steps as you go along.

Lastly, try to communicate each musical example. Ask yourself, What do I want to communicate to the audience in this piece of music? No matter how good your technique is, you will be unconvincing if you do not convey the meaning and mood of each piece.

As an ensemble member, respond to the person conducting, sing or play out, and follow the tempo given. Hold your music up and maintain eye contact. If you practice your conducting while seated, however tempting it may be, you will confuse the conductor and show that you are not actively participating in the group.

GUIDED PRACTICE

1. Warm up with group practice of *Finlandia, O Beautiful,* and/or "Break Forth."

2. Ask any last-minute questions at this point.

VIDEOTAPING #5—THEME FROM *FINLANDIA* (Sibelius), *O BEAUTIFUL FOR SPACIOUS SKIES* (Ward), AND/OR "BREAK FORTH, O BEAUTEOUS HEAVENLY LIGHT" (Bach)

ASSIGNMENT

1. View Videotaping #5, complete Evaluation Form V on both sides, and turn it in to the instructor.

2. Continue the practice of all elements of ambidextrous conducting. *O Beautiful* and/or "Break Forth" will be on the final conducting exam.

3. Read Lesson 20 in preparation for the next class session.

Name _____   Date ___/___/___   ┌──────┬──────┐
                                                              │   │   │
                                                              └──────┴──────┘
                                                                  Grades

EVALUATION FORM V

Complete the self-evaluation below. Leave those elements blank that are basically correct; use + for very good elements and − for elements that need improving.

Posture—Arm/Hand Positioning

_____ posture   _____ arm/hand positioning

Preparation

_____ mental set   _____ correct tempo

_____ group scan   _____ correct dynamic level

_____ smooth preparatory gesture   _____ correct articulation

_____ rhythmic breathing motion   _____ clear ictus

_____ eye contact   _____ confident and assuring demeanor

Patterns and Releases

_____ vertical plane location   _____ pattern clarity

_____ vertical plane amplitude   _____ internal releases

_____ horizontal plane location   _____ final release

_____ horizontal breadth   _____ release preparation

_____ clear ictus on each beat   _____ communication

Baton Grip and Use

_____ proper contact points   _____ baton on vertical plane

_____ natural curve of fingers   _____ ictus at baton tip

_____ correct direction of baton   _____ ictus on horizontal plane

Left Hand

_____ at-rest position: side   _____ appropriate dynamics

_____ at-rest position: front   _____ *crescendo-decrescendo*

_____ attention position   _____ appropriate releases

_____ smooth and independent   _____ sustaining gestures

Evaluation Summary. Summarize your conducting evaluation in narrative form. Write one paragraph summarizing the positive elements of your conducting and one paragraph on those elements that need improving.

Summarize positive elements:

Summarize those elements in need of improvement:

- ◼ Subdivision
- ◼ Cues
- ◼ Alto and Tenor Clefs

The basic gestures for the left hand have now been introduced, but they must be practiced daily if they are to become automatic. A convincing conducting technique is one that looks natural and responds to the music automatically, thus allowing the conductor to think about the music and not the gesture itself.

Objectives for this lesson are

- ● learning to conduct subdivision
- ● group cueing with the left hand
- ● applying new techniques to musical examples
- ● knowledge of alto and tenor clefs

GUIDED PRACTICE

1. Elect conductors to lead the class in the Circle Drill.

2. Review briefly any problems that were apparent in conducting *O Beautiful* and/or "Break Forth."

SUBDIVISION

Music that moves at a very slow tempo often requires a subdivision of beats in the conducting gesture. This helps to maintain rhythmic accuracy throughout and precision during a *ritardando,* especially in cadences.

The most common type of subdivided gesture is executed with a small rebound of the ictus and an additional ictus (the "and" of the beat) placed nearly in the same position as the primary beat (Figure 20.1). If the rebound of the primary ictus is too large, the following subdivision of the beat will look like a primary beat and not a subdivision. Keep the rebound of the primary ictus small by using little forearm action. The subdivided ictus is then made mostly with wrist action. This makes the subdivision look smaller and identifies it as a subdivided beat. This style is particularly useful when conducting music designated as *staccato.*

Used for very slow works/passages or rhythmic clarity

Figure 20.1 Rebound Subdivided Pattern

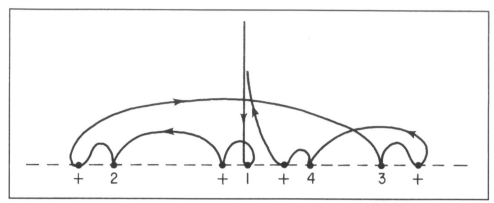

The rebound style of subdivided conducting also may be used for conducting passages of *hemiola,* an effect common in Baroque music in which the rhythmic organization in triple meter changes to a feeling of duple (3:2 relationship) without an actual meter change. Two measures of triple meter combine to have a "supermetric" quality of one measure in six (Figure 20.2). Because a primary accent shifts to beats three and two respectively, a subdivided three pattern may be used to indicate the hemiola. If a subdivided pattern is not used, then the gesture for the three pattern must show a shift in accentuation to communicate the rhythmic change.

A second type of gesture is used when the music has a greater flow but still requires subdivision. Rather than rebounding, each primary ictus makes a slight pause on the beat before traveling to the next beat (Figure 20.3). This "stop-start" action marks the primary beat at the "stop," and the subdivision of the beat at the "start." In Figure 20.3, the double slash stands for the pause of the primary ictus before the motion continues. This flowing rebound style is useful in conducting final cadences in Baroque music, where a *ritardando* is implied by a subdivision of the beats.

Conducting *marcato* articulation with subdivision is similar to conducting regular *marcato*. However, instead of a quick rebound motion that stops before moving to the next primary beat, the motion for a subdivided beat stops on the primary ictus, rebounds with a deep V angle and stops again before moving to the next ictus (Figure 20.4). This style of *marcato* "stop-stop" gesture is used for very slow and heavily accented passages of music.

Figure 20.2 Rebound Subdivision for Hemiola

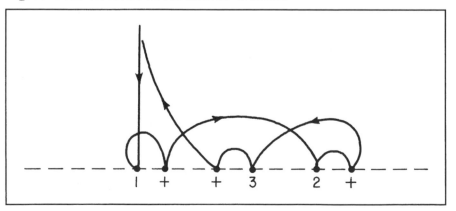

Figure 20.3 Flowing (Stop-Start) Subdivision

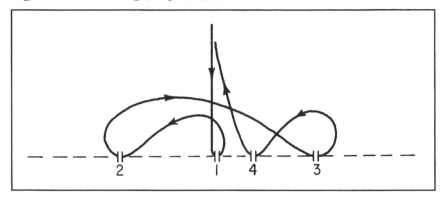

Figure 20.4 *Marcato* (Stop-Stop) Subdivision

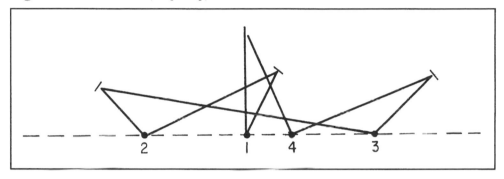

GUIDED PRACTICE

1. Practice each of the styles for subdivided conducting: (1) rebound, (2) flowing (stop-start), and (3) *marcato* (stop-stop).

2. Practice each of the styles for conducting two bars of hemiola: (1) subdivided, and (2) regular pattern with shifted accents.

CUES

"Surely He Hath Borne Out Griefs" (*Messiah*) by G. F. Handel

Handel's famous oratorio *Messiah* is one of the most popular Baroque compositions ever written. This excerpt from "Surely He Hath Borne Our Griefs" is one of the great movements for chorus and orchestra, and requires a rebound type of subdivided conducting. Notice that Handel indicated the character as *Largo e staccato,* with a dynamic level of *forte.* One rarely sees the combination of *staccato* articulation and loud dynamics, but the sharpness of the rhythm for the orchestra requires just such an approach. The metronome marking in parentheses is editorial; the eighth note indicates that the pulse is subdivided.

The left hand is used to conduct the chorus, and the right hand/baton conducts the orchestra. The left hand is not needed until measure six and remains down at the side until beat three of measure five, when it is raised to the "attention" position in preparation for cueing the chorus in measure six.

The right hand preparatory gesture must be rather forceful and "snap" to indicate the *staccato* nature of the jagged rhythms. A combination of wrist action and strong forearm movement will convey this style. The preparatory ictus is the "and" of beat four, but it is conducted like a regular preparatory gesture in common time.

Example 20.1 "Surely He Hath Borne Our Griefs" from *Messiah*

G. F. Handel

(Keep left-hand baton going for orchestra)

However, it is necessary to think of the preparatory ictus as the "and" of the beat to have the mental set for subdivided conducting.

The right hand/baton conducts a subdivided four pattern in rebound style throughout. The excerpt being conducted ends on the downbeat of measure twelve, and the conducting gesture stops on the downbeat.

Measure six provides the first cueing gesture for the left hand, and it is a full-ensemble cue—that is, the left hand moves directly forward to indicate a cue for the entire chorus. Cueing gestures move out at chest height and beyond the regular conducting area so as to be emphasized and seen.

The cueing motion is prepared on the beat prior to the cue, in this case, the "and" of beat four of measure five. At the same time as the preparation, eye contact must be made with the person or persons being cued. Eye contact that arrives on the cue is too late; ensemble members must find confidence for their entrance before the actual entrance takes place.

For "Surely," the left hand lifts slightly from the "attention" position on the "and" of beat four in measure five to indicate the preparatory breath. Simultaneously, eye contact is made, and the conductor breathes with the ensemble. The left hand is then thrust forward (hand open with thumb up) on beat one of measure six to cue the chorus on their entrance. The chorus is released on beat two with a small C cutoff (hand extended), lifts on the "and" of beat two (breath) and thrusts forward again for the cue on beat three. The left hand releases the choir on beat three with a small C cutoff and simultaneous breath. The left hand is then lifted on the "and" of beat four to cue the choir for the words "He hath."

The passage "He hath borne our griefs, and carried our sorrows," is heard, and may be conducted one of two ways. The phrase may be ended at "sorrows" with an internal cutoff on the "and" of beat four. The cutoff then becomes the preparation for the next forward cue on "Surely."

Some conductors prefer to maintain the energy of the phrase, carrying "sorrows" into "Surely" with no break between the words; this can be quite expressive. Direct the chorus to sing "sorrow,"

Example 20.1a Instrumental Parts for "Surely He Hath Borne Our Griefs"

Largo e staccato (♪ = 92)

omitting the final "s(z)," and sing forward to "Surely" with no breath between the words. The left hand is used to sustain the chorus through this long phrase. After the cue on "He hath" (measure six) the left hand pulls back toward the body and begins to move with the forward sustaining gesture (review Example 17.2). It is helpful to the chorus if the left hand lightly pulses the rhythm of the words as it moves forward. These must be subtle pulses, and the hand must inch forward very slowly so that it arrives extended (never fully extended with a straight arm) at the peak of the phrase on "sorrows." The preparation for the downbeat cue in measure nine

("Surely") is given on the "and" of beat four in measure nine by lifting the hand, as was done in measure five. Measures nine through eleven are conducted the same as measures six–eight, with the exception of a downstroke cutoff on the downbeat of measure twelve.

The conducting gestures for the opening of this chorus need to be intense, communicating the anguish and despair of the crucifixion. The cueing of the left hand should be forceful, indicating the *forte* dynamic level. The right hand/baton must maintain an even subdivision of the beat while communicating the jagged rhythmic quality.

GUIDED PRACTICE

1. Practice conducting the subdivided pattern in unison. Remember to use less forearm motion on the rebound of the primary beat, with the subdivided beat being indicated mostly by the wrist.

2. Practice the left hand cueing and sustaining gestures for the chorus.

3. Practice the ambidextrous conducting of "Surely." Memorize the music quickly (twelve measures) in order that eye contact may be maintained with the ensemble.

"Air" from *Orchestral Suite No. 3 in D Major* by J. S. Bach

This famous "Air" from Bach's third orchestral suite (Example 20.2) is another example of music at a very slow tempo that will be clearer with a subdivided beat pattern. The steady division of the pulse in the bass line of the continuo part must be precise if the players are to stay together.

Because of the quiet delicacy of this movement, the subdivision must be gentle, with very little rebound at all. This example may be conducted with the right hand only, and for the sake of time the repeats may be omitted. There are no cutoffs except at the end of each complete section.

GUIDED PRACTICE

1. If there is a sufficient number of string players, play the "Air" while the instructor conducts. If not, singers may sing the melody on "du" an octave lower than written, and other instruments may take the other parts.

2. Practice the "Air" as a group while singing the melody an octave lower on "du." Monitor for a gentle subdivision of the beat and very *legato* phrasing (just the opposite of "Surely").

Example 20.2 "Air" from *Orchestral Suite No. 3 in D Major*   **J. S. Bach**

ALTO AND TENOR CLEFS

Not all instruments play from the treble or bass clef, the most common clefs used today. In fact, music of earlier times used a variety of clefs, even for the different vocal parts. Examples of these can be seen in the opening of the chorale "O Sacred Head Now Wounded," as harmonized by J. S. Bach (Example 20.3). The old-style vocal score shows a different soprano clef, alto clef, tenor clef, and bass clef. The soprano, alto, and tenor clefs are C clefs, in which the note on the staff indicated by the clef is middle C. For the soprano clef, middle C is the first line; for the alto clef, the third line; and for the tenor clef, the fourth. These clefs were used to enable most of the notes for each vocal part to be placed on the staff, eliminating the excessive use of ledger lines.

Today, a system of four clefs remains in use: treble, alto, tenor, and bass. Vocal music uses only two clefs, treble and bass, as shown in Example 20.3. The tenor part uses the treble clef (notes sounding an octave lower) when it is written in open score, for which each vocal part has its own staff. When written in closed score (e.g., a hymn), the tenor part appears with the bass part in the bass clef.

Instrumental parts are written in all four clefs. The alto clef is also known as the viola clef, since it is used most consistently in music for the viola. As mentioned, this clef places middle C on the third line of the staff (Example 20.4). This is not considered a transposition; all notes are at concert pitch. Knowing the position of middle C makes it possible to designate all other pitches of the scales.

The tenor clef, in which middle C is placed on the fourth line of the staff, is shown in Example 20.5. No instrument uses the tenor clef consistently. However, trombone, cello, and bassoon parts often are found written in the tenor clef when a musical passage is in the higher register.

Conductors of instrumental music must be able to read both alto and tenor clefs with ease. Such a skill is not required for this course, but students should understand the basic theory of how alto and tenor clefs designate pitches.

Example 20.3 Old and New Vocal Styles

Old Style Vocal Score

New Style Vocal Score

Example 20.4 Alto Clef and Pitch Designations

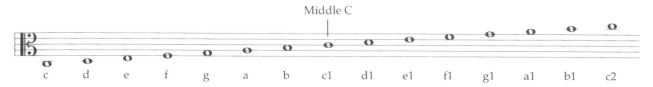

Middle C

c   d   e   f   g   a   b   c1   d1   e1   f1   g1   a1   b1   c2

Example 20.5 Tenor Clef and Pitch Designations

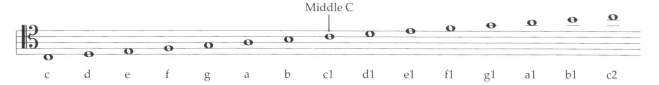

Middle C

c   d   e   f   g   a   b   c1   d1   e1   f1   g1   a1   b1   c2

ASSIGNMENT

1. Continue to practice all left hand conducting techniques, including the Circle Drill.

2. Practice the three styles of subdivided conducting: rebound, flowing, and *marcato.*

3. Practice the excerpt of "Surely He Hath Borne Our Griefs," with right hand/baton only. Monitor for a *forte* yet *staccato*-like gesture that conveys Handel's designation *Largo e staccato.* Now practice the excerpt with left hand only. Monitor for a forceful cueing action and a subtle sustaining gesture. Finally, practice using both hands. Remember the breathing motion, and don't forget to maintain eye contact with the choir.

4. Practice the "Air" from Bach's third orchestral suite. Maintain a gentle and flowing pattern with the right hand/baton that conveys the subtle subdivision of this music.

5. Study the material on alto and tenor clefs for a quiz in the next class session. Also, study the viola part to the "Air." Can you make sense of it? Conductors of instrumental ensembles must become facile with the alto clef.

6. Read Lesson 21 in preparation for the next class session.

■ Composer's Intent
■ Listener's Response

You should be feeling more comfortable with the use of the left hand by now. Continue to practice drills with each hand separately and then together.

Objectives for this lesson are
- more expressive conducting and interpretation
- greater confidence with ambidextrous conducting

COMPOSER'S INTENT

It has been stressed frequently that the most important role of the conductor is to communicate to the ensemble the "spirit" of the music; merely playing notes inspires no one. Yet it is a common experience, even among professional musicians. And for the audience, how boring it is to listen to music that is dull and unmoving. The conductor must be able to move the ensemble beyond the musical page to capture the composer's musical intent. Truly great performances transport the listener beyond the purely intellectual (although intellect is not to be discounted) to a level of experience that transcends the mundane and ordinary. It should be the desire of every musician and conductor to communicate "feelingful" interpretations of the world's greatest music.

Such a musical experience rarely just happens; it requires much study and preparation of the musical score by conductor and ensemble alike. The overall design of each composition must be understood, as well as the focal points. All of the dynamic indications, tempos, articulations, phrasing, etc., must be studied and understood for the contribution each makes to the expressive qualities of the music. This takes times and a willingness to analyze beyond the superficial. Great music is great because there is always more to learn each time it is returned to and studied.

LISTENER'S RESPONSE

Perhaps the two most important questions a conductor must ask are Why is this piece worth performing? and What is the intended listener response? If the conductor cannot answer the first question, he or she will have no idea how to answer the second. While many personal and subjective preferences may enter into answering the first question, there are structural and technical guidelines that help the conductor to determine the value placed on a piece of music. These are the elements studied in musical analysis classes. The intended listener response, however, is a decision that is guided more by one's own instincts and feelings; successful conductors must be able to communicate a wide range of emotions.

The musical compositions used in this course are purposely not complex. The simplest piece of music, however, does have a "spirit" that will come to life if the conductor perceives and communicates its "message." Therefore, the conductor must ask the two questions above before conducting each composition. While people may respond or react differently to a given piece of music, and while there is no right or wrong interpretation, there should be an interpretation in the conductor's mind that is guiding the direction of the ensemble. If little thought is given to musical meaning, even a technically proficient performance will be dull and void of life.

Professional musicians often fall into the routine of "making" music—churning out the notes with little thought given to creating music that is emotionally and intellectually stimulating. The conductor of an ensemble has the responsibility to motivate, inspire, and lead the members in re-creating something that has life and meaning for the audience. This process begins long before the first rehearsal, with forethought and study. When carried through to its end, the process culminates in a meaningful and satisfying musical experience for the audience and the ensemble. For music to have life, it must first "live" in the musician.

As a conductor, you must ask yourself, "Do I look the part?" Much as an actor conveys a different identity by assuming the personality of and physical characteristics of the person being played, so must the conductor convey the "personality" of each musical score. This is done by subtle changes in the physical stance (such as standing tall to communicate power and strength), the style of the conducting gesture, and very important, facial expression. The conductor's face must be as "active" as that of the mime who conveys a message without words.

Now that your conducting gestures are (or should be) becoming more natural and automatic, work more on conveying the "meaning and mood" of each composition. Study yourself in a mirror and via the class videotapings to see if you "look" on the outside the way you "feel" on the inside. If not, work on varying your physical gestures and expressions in an overt manner until you find the "look" that conveys the message.

Conducting the excerpts from "Surely He Hath Borne Our Griefs" (Handel) and the "Air" by Bach provides excellent opportunities to communicate deeply moving pieces of music. But first you must ask, "What was the composer's intent?" and then, "What response do I want from the listeners?" Answering both of these questions should guide you to a meaningful interpretation. The important points to remember are, no matter what your interpretation, *have one,* and *communicate it* to the ensemble.

GUIDED PRACTICE

1. Practice a "mime" exercise in which you do (reflect) exactly what your instructor does in assuming various postures for such responses as: happiness, anger, melancholy, scolding, sadness. Combine these looks with conducting patterns that also reflect these emotions.

2. Practice "eyebrow sit-ups," or raising and lowering of the eyebrows. Make the biggest face possible (dropped jaw with eyes opened wide), followed by the smallest face possible (pursed lips, furrowed brow). Note how important facial expression is to effective conducting.

3. Review the rebound, subdivided conducting used for "Surely He Hath Borne Our Griefs" and the "Air."

4. Review the left hand gestures for cueing and sustaining used for "Surely He Hath Borne Our Griefs."

5. Practice "Surely" with ambidextrous conducting. When instrumental forces are lacking, a recorded example of the first twelve bars is helpful in this practice, although the preparatory gesture will not be possible to execute in time with the beginning of the recorded excerpt. You must play "catch-up" with the recording on the first or second beats.

6. If time permits, you may elect to conduct the class in "Surely" (Example 20.1) and/or the "Air" (Example 20.2).

ASSIGNMENT

1. Practice the Circle Drill to achieve hand independence.

2. Practice various facial postures and physical stances to relay different emotions.

3. Study the excerpt from "Surely He Hath Borne Our Griefs" to determine the composer's intent, and decide upon a listener response and a means by which you will communicate this desired response. Practice the excerpt first with the right hand, then with the left, then together.

4. Study the "Air" by Bach; this is nonreferential music, but there is a "spirit" or feeling in the music that is so beautiful. How will you convey this emotion in your conducting gesture? Practice the pattern with the right hand until it is fluid. Now, can you use the left hand to help shape the phrasing?

5. Read Lesson 22 in preparation for the next class session.

Lesson 22

- Entrances on Incomplete Beats
- Instrumental Transpositions: C and B-flat

Are you still feeling nervous when you conduct the ensemble? Try focusing upon the music and not yourself. Also, remember to use anxious feelings to motivate you in a positive direction.

Objectives for this lesson are
- executing entrances on pickup notes
- further refinement of left hand usage
- transpositions in C and B-flat

ENTRANCES ON INCOMPLETE BEATS

Music often begins on a note value that is less than a full beat in duration, such as an eighth note in common time. Such entrances are prepared and conducted as though they were on the beat. Therefore, the two examples in Example 22.1 are prepared and conducted identically; the preparatory ictus is beat three, the downbeat is given, and the ensemble will begin either on beat one or the "and" of beat one, whichever they are playing/singing.

Example 22.1 Identical Preparations for Entrances on and after the Beat

A. Entrance on Beat

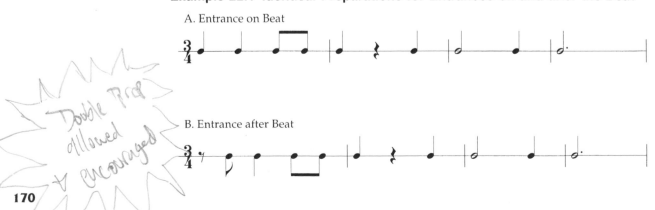

B. Entrance after Beat

170

If a full beat of rest occurs on the downbeat at the beginning of a composition, this will be given as the preparatory ictus. However, preparatory gestures are never given with a downward movement, as this negates the breathing motion. Therefore, the preparatory gesture will rise on beat one, but in the opposite direction of beat two. The first measure in Example 22.2 is conducted the same as the opening to the theme from *Finlandia* (Example 17.1), except in *Finlandia* no rest is given on the first beat. Whether the rest is shown on beat one, or whether the music just begins on beat two, the preparatory ictus is the same—beat one.

When more than one beat of rest occurs before the first note of a composition, the conductor must account for every beat that is notated. The preparatory ictus will be the best (rest) that immediately precedes the first note, and the preparatory gesture will be given in the opposite direction of the first note. Beats of rest that precede the preparatory ictus (rest) are indicated by the conductor as "marking beats," or small downbeats that are visible to the ensemble. Because no preparatory gesture is given prior to these marking beats, players will not enter by mistake. In Example 22.3, the first two rests are marking beats, the rest on beat three is the preparatory ictus, and the preparatory gesture is given like that for a normal pickup in common time—left to right.

Example 22.2 Preparation for One Beat of Rest before First Note

Example 22.3 Marking on Beats One and Two

Pickup notes are often less than a full beat in duration. The preparatory gesture is not given for the pickup note(s), but rather the downbeat that follows. In this case, the pickup note becomes part of the preparatory gesture.

If the tempo is moderate to slow, the preparatory gesture can be subdivided by pausing on the upward movement and continuing upward for the pickup note(s). The beat note in Example 22.4 (*It Came upon the Midnight Clear*) is the dotted quarter; the eighth-note pickup is, therefore, less than a full beat in duration. Because the tempo is rather slow, a normal preparation is given for duple meter, the preparatory gesture pauses as it rises, then continues on with a lift of the hand/baton to indicate the pickup. In this case, the pickup is still conducted as part of the preparatory gesture.

Example 22.4 Entrance on a Fraction of a Beat in Slow Tempo:
It Came upon the Midnight Clear

R. S. Willis

Example 22.5 Entrance on Fraction of a Beat in Fast Tempo:
The Farmer in the Dell   **English Singing Game**

In Example 22.5 (*The Farmer in the Dell*), the beat note again is the dotted quarter, but the tempo is fast. The eighth-note pickup occurs too quickly for a subdivision of the preparatory gesture. Therefore, the pickup note occurs simultaneously with the quick action of the preparation, which is not subdivided.

Example 22.6 (*La Marseillaise*) begins with a sixteenth note as a pickup to beat four. In this case, the preparatory ictus is beat three, a part of which becomes the sixteenth-note pickup. The preparatory gesture is given left to right as for a regular one-beat pickup in common time; the beginning sixteenth note occurs following the breath at the end of the preparatory gesture.

Remember this summary regarding pickup notes of less than a full beat in duration: If the music does not start on the count, but on a fractional value, ignore the fraction and give the same rhythmic preparation that you would if the music began on the next full count. Do not try to beat the fractions, but rather feel them within the regular preparatory gesture.

Example 22.6 Entrance on Fraction of a Beat in Fast Tempo: *La Marseillaise*
R. de Lisle

GUIDED PRACTICE

1. Practice each of the examples in Examples 22.1–22.6 in unison, following your instructor's model.

2. State the directive regarding the preparation of notes less than a full beat in duration.

3. Practice the right hand and left hand gestures separately and then together for "Surely He Hath Borne Our Griefs." If time permits, you may conduct the class in the excerpt individually.

4. Practice the conducting of the "Air" by Bach (optional). If time permits, you may conduct the class individually in this piece.

INSTRUMENTAL TRANSPOSITIONS: C AND B-FLAT

Not all instruments actually produce or sound the note that is written for them. These are called transposing instruments, which means the notes they see and play are not written in concert pitch. The transposed parts for these instruments are written at a set interval above or below the pitch that actually sounds (concert pitch, or key of the composition). Transposing instruments are the result of an evolving process of instrument development that resulted in the shape and length of the instrument dictating its natural harmonic series. In order for some instruments to play in the same key as other instruments, transposition became necessary to adjust the tuning of the instruments to concert pitch.

Conducting instrumental music requires that conductors understand the relationship of transposed parts to concert pitch and be facile with this knowledge when studying scores. The latter is not an objective of this course, but the beginning conducting student does need to understand in theory how transposition works and which instruments transpose.

A number of instruments are "C transposing," that is, the written notes sound in the same key, but up or down one or more octaves (Example 22.7). The C-transposing instruments that sound one octave higher than written are the piccolo in C, celesta, and bell lyra. The orchestral bells are also a C-transposing instrument, but sound two octaves higher than written. The guitar, string bass, and contrabassoon are C-transposing instruments that sound an octave lower than written.

Example 22.7 Table of Transpositions for C Instruments

Instruments	Sound		Written	Sounds
C Piccolo Bell Lyra Celesta Xylophone	One Octave Higher			
Orchestra Bells	Two Octaves Higher			
Guitar String Bass Contrabassoon	One Octave Lower			

B-flat instruments sound a major 2nd, major 9th, or major 16th lower than written. In other words, when B-flat instruments read a written concert C they may sound the pitch B-flat one whole step below, an octave and a step below, or two octaves and a step below. In order for B-flat instruments to sound in the concert key, the parts must be transposed or written in a key signature a major 2nd above the concert key. In Example 22.8, the B-flat clarinet part is written in the key of D major in order to sound in the concert key of C major.

The B-flat transposing instruments that sound a major 2nd lower than the written pitch are the B-flat clarinet, B-flat trumpet, B-flat cornet, fluegelhorn, and soprano saxophone. The bass clarinet, tenor saxophone, and treble clef euphonium are B-flat instruments that sound a major 9th lower than written. B-flat instruments that sound a major 16th lower than written are the BB-flat contrabass clarinet, and the bass saxophone (Example 22.9).

Example 22.8 Written Part for B-flat Clarinet Sounding in C Major

B-flat Part

Written

Sounds

Example 22.9 Table of Transpositions for B-flat Instruments

Instruments	Sound		Written	Sounds
B-flat Clarinet B-flat Trumpet B-flat Cornet Fluegelhorn Soprano Saxophone	Major 2nd Lower			
Bass Clarinet Tenor Saxophone Euphonium	Major 9th Lower			
BB-flat Contrabass Clarinet Bass Saxophone	Major 16th Lower			

GUIDED PRACTICE

1. As the instructor chooses transposing instruments in the C and B-flat classifications, and writes a note on the staff (chalkboard) for that instrument in a chosen key (the instrument's written part), determine the correct key and concert pitch for each example.

2. As the instructor chooses transposing instruments in the C and B-flat classifications, and writes a note on the staff (chalkboard) for that instrument in a chosen concert key (pitch that is sounding), determine the key and pitch for the transposed part.

ASSIGNMENT

1. Practice the excerpt from "Surely He Hath Borne Our Griefs" and/or the "Air" by Bach for individual conducting and videotaping in the next class session.

2. Continue to practice all elements of ambidextrous conducting.

3. Review and practice Examples 22.1–22.6 to understand entrances on incomplete beats.

4. Study the materials in Instrumental Transpositions: C and B-flat, for a quiz in the next class session.

5. Read Lesson 23 in preparation for the next class session.

■ Videotaping #6

① 1-2
② 4-1
③ 2-3
④ 2-1

You should be feeling more comfortable with maintaining hand independence if you are practicing daily.

Objectives of this sixth videotaping lesson are

- habitual posture and arm/hand positioning
- habitual preparatory set and clear preparatory gesture
- habitual eye contact and rhythmic breathing motion
- subdivided patterns that are clearly delineated by the right hand/baton
- confident and independent use of the left hand in sustaining, cueing, and dynamic gestures
- a confident and assuring demeanor
- a meaningful and appropriate interpretation

Preparation

Read the elements that will be evaluated in this sixth videotaping as found on Evaluation Form VI in this lesson. This will serve as a review of all gestures and techniques studied thus far. Review the videotape of your conducting and follow the directives as to the use of the form. Pay close attention to the constructive comments that the instructor has made on the tape, which will help you to complete the self-evaluation form.

When it is your turn to conduct, proceed to the conductor's stand, place your music on it, and fix the tempo in your mind *before* raising your head and arm. Once you are set to begin, raise your head and arm simultaneously, scan the group with your eyes, give the preparatory gesture with rhythmic breathing motion, and keep your eyes up on the downbeat. If something goes wrong with your conducting at the very beginning, stop and begin again. Remember, initial nervousness will sometimes cause a bad start. If, however, you lose your place or the pattern falters during the music—keep going! **Remember: do not advertise your mistakes!**

Lastly, work to interpret the musical example. What is it that you want to communicate? No matter how good your technique is, you will be unconvincing if you do not convey the meaning and mood of each piece.

GUIDED PRACTICE

1. Warm up with group practice of "Surely He Hath Borne Our Griefs" and/or the "Air" by Bach. If a pianist is available, it is suggested that he or she play the piano accompaniment of the reduced orchestral parts of "Surely." Available string players may play from the instrumental parts provided. The remainder of the ensemble may then choose a vocal part to sing or double with an instrument (parts provided). Because the vocal parts are a little difficult, the instructor may wish to have you conduct to a recording, which means that you will not be able to give an accurate preparatory gesture. While the use of a recording may not be desirable, it will give you a more accurate representation of the actual sound, especially when the class size is small.

2. Ask the instructor any last-minute questions at this time.

VIDEOTAPING #6—"SURELY HE HATH BORNE OUR GRIEFS" (Handel) AND/OR "AIR" (Bach)

ASSIGNMENT

1. View Videotaping #6, complete Evaluation Form VI on both sides, and return it to the instructor.

2. Continue the practice of all elements of ambidextrous conducting.

3. Read Lesson 24 in preparation for the next class session.

Name _____   Date ____/____/____   [|]
                                                                      Grades

EVALUATION FORM VI

Complete the self-evaluation below. Leave those elements blank that are basically correct; use + for very good elements and − for elements that need improving.

Posture—Arm/Hand Positioning

_____ posture   _____ arm/hand positioning

Preparation

_____ mental set   _____ correct tempo

_____ group scan   _____ correct dynamic level

_____ smooth preparatory gesture   _____ correct articulation

_____ rhythmic breathing motion   _____ clear ictus

_____ eye contact   _____ confident and assuring demeanor

Patterns and Releases

_____ vertical plane location   _____ pattern clarity

_____ vertical plane amplitude   _____ internal releases

_____ horizontal plane location   _____ final release

_____ horizontal breadth   _____ release preparation

_____ clear ictus on each beat   _____ communication

Baton Grip and Use

_____ proper contact points   _____ baton on vertical plane

_____ natural curve of fingers   _____ ictus at baton tip

_____ correct direction of baton   _____ ictus on horizontal plane

Left Hand

_____ at-rest position: side   _____ appropriate dynamics

_____ at-rest position: front   _____ *crescendo-decrescendo*

_____ attention position   _____ appropriate releases

_____ smooth and independent   _____ sustaining gestures

Evaluation Summary. Summarize your conducting evaluation in narrative form. Write one paragraph summarizing the positive elements of your conducting and one paragraph on those elements that need improving.

Summarize positive elements:

Summarize those elements in need of improvement:

Lesson 24

- ■ Fermatas
- ■ Compound Meters: Six, Nine, Twelve
- ■ Instrumental Transpositions: F, E-flat, A

This lesson adds two more techniques to your ever growing vocabulary of conducting gestures.

Objectives for this lesson are
- learning to conduct three types of fermatas
- conducting compound meters in six, nine, twelve
- applying new techniques to musical examples
- continuing to refine all conducting techniques

FERMATAS

The *fermata* (hold) requires that the rhythmic movement stop and notes of the music be held on the beat where the fermata is indicated. How long the notes are held is at the interpretive discretion of the conductor. While the fermata is being sustained, it is recommended that either the right hand, left hand, or both remain in slow motion to indicate that the music is being sustained. This movement of hands should occur in a horizontal, right- and/or leftward direction (slow, horizontal sweep); care must be taken not to raise the hands lest the ensemble think that a *crescendo* is being indicated (unless, of course, it is).

There are three types of fermatas that the student must learn to conduct: (1) the long-break fermata; (2) the short-break fermata; and (3) the no-break, or continued, fermata. These designations have little to do with the length of the fermata, but everything to do with what follows it.

When a fermata is followed by a rest or complete break (*caesura*), it is of the long-break style. The release of this type of fermata is like a final release, followed by a period of silence. A new preparatory gesture must then be given for the note on which the music resumes. Notice in Example 24.1 that the fermata on beat three is followed by a double slash (caesura), the symbol that indicates a complete break. The length of the break like the length of the fermata is at the discretion of the conductor. The quarter rest on beat four following the fermata is then used as the preparatory ictus for the downbeat of the next measure. In the diagram in Figure 24.1, the thick horizontal line beginning at beat three indicates the length of the fermata or hold. The cutoff to the right stops for a period of silence, which is then followed by another rightward movement (dotted line) for the new preparation.

A fermata that is followed by a short pause, as in Example 24.2, is of the second type of fermata (short break). The release of this fermata becomes the same gesture for preparing the next beat upon which the music begins again. As with other internal cutoffs, the release and the breath occur simultaneously. Therefore, the "break" between the fermata and the beginning of the next phrase is the time it takes for a breath at the tempo needed to resume the flow of the music. As with other internal releases, the tail of this short-break cutoff must conclude in an upward direction for the following beat to be directed downward to the horizontal plane (Figure 24.2).

The no-break fermata (Example 24.3) is one in which there is no pause following the fermata, not even for a breath. The fermata is held at the discretion of the conductor, then the music moves on to the next phrase without a break.

We have learned that changes in dynamics and articulation must be communicated to the ensemble by adequate preparation. The same is true of the fermata that continues directly on to the next phrase—some type of preparation must be given to indicate that the music is to resume. In this case, the movement of the preparation is a continuation of the beat being held; it moves in the same direction as the beat on which the hold has been slowly moving (Figure 24.3). The preparation is seen as being different from the holding movement in that the preparation moves at the speed at which the music is being resumed.

Figure 24.1 Long-Break Fermata

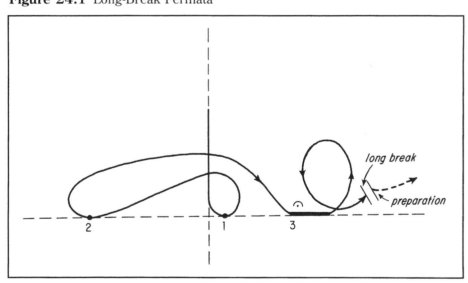

Example 24.1 Long-Break Fermata

Figure 24.2 Short-Break Fermata

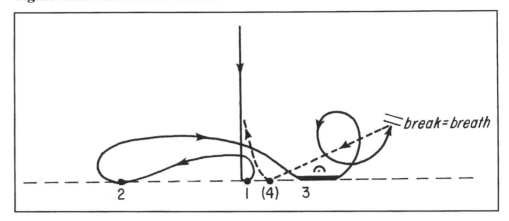

Example 24.2 Short-Break Fermata

Figure 24.3 No-Break Fermata

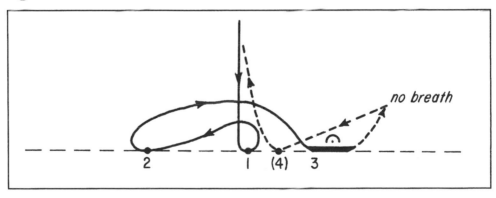

Example 24.3 No-Break Fermata

GUIDED PRACTICE

1. Observe the instructor model each of the three fermata styles, and practice in unison.

2. Conduct the fermatas in the last part of the *Star-Spangled Banner* (Example 24.4) using all three styles of fermata. What type of fermata is used traditionally for the singing of these phrases? What type of fermata would be appropriate if a dramatic effect were desired on the word "free"? Why would the no-break fermata be the least likely to be used?

Example 24.4 *The Star-Spangled Banner*

J. S. Smith

COMPOUND METERS: SIX, NINE, TWELVE

Compound meters differ from simple meters in that the beat note for simple meters (two, three, four) is divisible by two, while that of compound meters (six, nine, twelve) is divisible by three. Compound meters are not to be thought of as subdivisions, for in compound meters each beat is a unit unto itself, and not part of any other beat.

The conducting pattern for compound meters that move at a fast tempo will be the same as those for conducting simple meters (six will be conducted in two, nine will be conducted in three, and twelve will be conducted in four). The underlying pulse, however, is still divisible by three. When the tempo is slow, however, each of the compound meters is conducted with its own pattern that clearly identifies each of the beats of the meter.

The classical six pattern is diagrammed in Figure 24.4. Note that each of the beats is equally placed and identified along the horizontal plane. Beginning conductors often bunch these beats together, a practice that is to be avoided. Notice that the rebound of beat three crosses over the vertical plane to beat four; the fourth ictus must not be located at the same location as beat one. Beat six also has its own designated location.

The classical nine pattern is diagrammed in Figure 24.5. The first three beats are placed the same as those of the six pattern. However, beats four, five, and six all move rightward, and beats seven, eight, and nine lift off the horizontal plane to come up the side of the vertical plane.

Lifting the last three beats from the horizontal plane helps to clarify the position of these beats when there are six beats occurring to the right of the vertical plane. Care must be taken that the rebounds of these last ictuses not loop around to the next beat, lest the ictus itself become lost in the rebound motion. Keep the in–out action very clear when conducting beats seven, eight, and nine.

The classical twelve pattern is diagrammed in Figure 24.6. Notice that beats two and three move to the right; this movement is confusing at first. Beats four, five, and six move to the left, and beats seven, eight, and nine move to the right. The ictuses for beats ten, eleven, and twelve move up the vertical plane as did the last three beats for the nine pattern.

More beats are indicated in compound patterns than in simple, and thus more opportunity for beats to bunch up, resulting in lack of clarity in the conducting gesture. Add the practice of these compound patterns to your daily rehearsal plan.

Figure 24.4 The Six Pattern

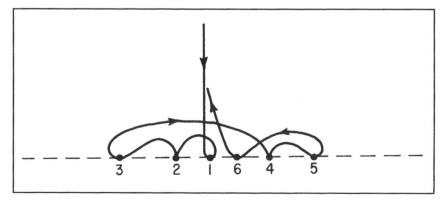

Figure 24.5 The Nine Pattern

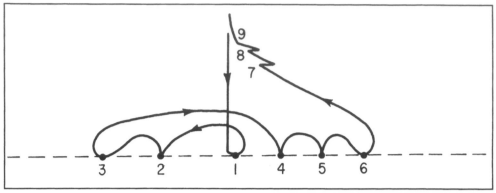

Figure 24.6 The Twelve Pattern

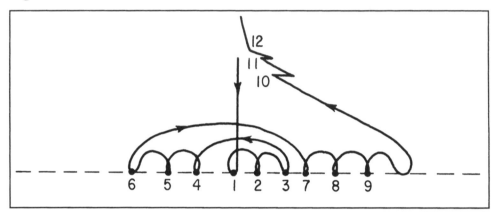

GUIDED PRACTICE

1. Observe the instructor model each of the three compound patterns, and practice in unison.

2. Practice the three compound patterns in succession, conducting four measures of each pattern as was done with the simple meters in the Daily Dozen exercise.

Silent Night by Franz Gruber

Silent Night (Example 24.5) is one of the world's most famous melodies. It is a good example for conducting the slow six pattern with the right hand/baton. Notice that internal cutoffs occur after every two measures; these releases will be indicated by the right hand/baton. Measure ten contains a *crescendo* with fermata (long break) for teaching purposes. The final release is on beat six in measure twelve.

The left hand is used to indicate dynamic levels and for sustaining purposes. In measure one, the left hand indicates a *piano* dynamic level. It changes to a forward sustaining gesture on beat three of measure one ("night"), moving forward to the downbeat of measure two to indicate a continuous phrase (no breath). On beat two of measure two, the left hand is withdrawn to the "attention" position.

The same sustaining movement is used by the left hand for measures three and four. Thereafter, the left hand is lowered to the side as it is not needed in measures five–eight. To mirror these measures is unnecessary conducting.

The left hand is raised to the "attention" position on the downbeat of measure eleven to prepare for its use to indicate the *crescendo* (palm up) in measure twelve. The rhythmic movement stops on measure twelve on the fermata; the left palm is up indicating the hold at the fermata. Both hands may pull slightly sideways to indicate the sustained quality of the fermata.

Both hands are used to release for the long break following the fermata, with the tails of the cutoffs moving in opposite directions. The hands

"freeze" in the air to denote the long break, and the last phrase of music is prepared with mirrored preparatory gestures. The left hand indicates the *decrescendo* in measure eleven as the right hand conducts the six pattern. The final measure can be sustained in the left hand while the right conducts the pattern, or both hands can sustain the final measure with five small marking beats and a mirrored release on beat six.

The character of *Silent Night* requires a subtle ictus and a very *legato* articulation. Practice floating across the horizontal plane with very little rebound and as smooth a gesture as possible.

Example 24.5 *Silent Night*   F. Gruber

GUIDED PRACTICE

1. Observe the instructor model the right hand gestures for *Silent Night*, and practice in unison.

2. Observe the instructor model the left hand gestures for *Silent Night*, and practice in unison. Monitor for withdrawal of the left hand sustaining gesture on beat two of measures two and four.

Example 24.5a Instrumental Parts for *Silent Night*

> 3. The *crescendo*, fermata, long break, and *decrescendo* gestures in measures eleven and twelve need to be practiced independently. As the instructor models these measures, practice in unison.
>
> 4. Practice *Silent Night* using ambidextrous conducting.

A Gaelic Melody (Traditional)

"A Gaelic Melody" (Example 24.6) is a supplemental selection for the practice of compound meter. The slow tempo requires a *legato* nine pattern. The melody begins on beat seven, the preparation for which begins at the center and moves rightward and upward with the

Example 24.6 "A Gaelic Melody"   Harm. D. Evans

baton. Beats seven, eight, and nine are then conducted upward on the vertical plane as shown in Figure 24.5. The internal cutoffs in measures two, four, and six all occur rightward and are simultaneous with the breath. This example can be conducted with the right hand/baton only.

"La Paix" (excerpt from *Royal Fireworks Music*) by G. F. Handel

"La Paix" or "Peace" (Example 24.7) is a supplemental selection for the practice of compound meter. (It has been slightly edited.) Singers may perform on a neutral syllable. It should be conducted at a slow tempo in the style of the "Siciliano," a seventeenth- and eighteenth-century dance type in 6/8 or 12/8 meter, with a flowing broken-chordal accompaniment and soft, lyrical melody with dotted rhythms.

GUIDED PRACTICE

1. Review with the instructor the nine pattern and conduct in unison. Group conducting of "A Gaelic Melody" will aid in developing a musically expressive nine pattern.

2. Review with the instructor the twelve pattern and conduct in unison. Group conducting of "La Paix" will aid in developing a musically expressive twelve pattern.

Example 24.7 "La Paix" from *Royal Fireworks Music*   G. F. Handel

INSTRUMENTAL TRANSPOSITIONS: F, E-FLAT, A

Instruments in F sound a perfect 5th lower than written. The key signature for the written part has one less flat (or one more sharp) than the concert key; it may also be thought of as the key signature a perfect 5th above the concert pitch. Thus, a composition written in the key of C major will have parts written in G major for the F transposing instruments (Example 24.8).

The horn in F and the English horn are the two instruments that commonly use the F transposition. Although F is the usual key for horn parts, they also appear in such keys as E-flat, A, D, E, G, and B-flat.

Transpositions in E-flat sound either a major 6th lower, or an octave plus a major 6th lower than written (Example 24.9). The written part uses the key signature a major 6th above the concert key. Thus, a composition written in the key of C major will have parts written in A major. Those E-flat transposing instruments that sound a major 6th lower than written are the alto saxophone and the alto clarinet.

Example 24.8 Transposed Part for F Instruments Sounding in C Major

F Part

Written

Sounds

192   BASIC TECHNIQUES OF CONDUCTING

Example 24.9 Table of Transpositions for E-flat Instruments

Instruments	Sound		Written	Sounds

Alto Clarinet
Alto Saxophone — Major 6th Lower

EE-flat Contra-alto
  Clarinet — Major 6th plus Octave Lower
Baritone Saxophone

E-flat Clarinet — Minor 3rd Higher

The EE-flat contralto clarinet and the baritone saxophone both sound an octave plus a major 6th lower, and the E-flat clarinet sounds a minor 3rd higher than written.

The clarinet in A is another transposing instrument. It sounds a minor 3rd lower than the written part. Other transposing instruments include the D trumpet (sounds a major 2nd higher), the B-flat piccolo trumpet (sound a minor 7th higher), and the D-flat piccolo (sounds an octave and a minor 2nd higher). Instruments that do not transpose are the flute, oboe, bassoon, C trumpet, trombone, tuba, violin, cello, marimba, chimes, vibraphone, and timpani.

ASSIGNMENT

1. Practice the three styles of conducting fermatas in Examples 24.1–24.3.

2. Practice the patterns for the compound meters: six, nine, twelve. Conduct these patterns in sets of Daily Dozens.

3. Practice *Silent Night* in six with the right hand only. Practice the left hand gestures, and combine both left and right hand gestures. This selection will be conducted before the class for Videotaping #7.

4. Read the material on Instrumental Transpositions: F, E-flat, A, for a quiz in the next class session.

5. Read Lesson 25 in preparation for the next class.

Lesson 25

■ Asymmetric Meters: Conducting in Five and Seven
■ Changing Meters

Contemporary music is replete with examples having asymmetric and/or changing meters. You should have at least a fundamental understanding of these conducting techniques.

Objectives for this lesson are
- learning to conduct in five and seven
- understanding changing meters
- conducting compound meters
- refining left hand conducting

ASYMMETRIC METERS: CONDUCTING IN FIVE AND SEVEN

Asymmetric meters have two characteristics in common: each contains an odd number of beats; and in faster tempos these meters consist of various beat notes of unequal length, the most common of which are groupings of twos and threes. Two of the most common asymmetric meters are those in five and seven. When music in these meters moves at a tempo from moderate to slow, the beat pattern will reflect either five or seven ictuses.

The slow asymmetric meter of five can be conducted in one of two ways, depending upon the rhythmical organization of the meter: 3 + 2 or 2 + 3. Figure 25.1 shows the diagram of the gesture for five when the rhythm is grouped 3 + 2. Notice that beats two and three are to the left of the vertical plane as in the six pattern.

The 2 + 3 organization of the five pattern is shown in Figure 25.2. Notice now that only beat two is placed to the left of the vertical plane, and beats three and four are placed to the right. In both diagrams, beat five is in the same position on the horizontal plane.

When the tempo of the music in five meter moves fast, the pattern reverts to duple, with one of the two beats "dragging" or longer. In the 3 + 2 pattern, the downstroke becomes the "drag" beat, and the conductor must count internally: 1-2-3. The gesture on beat two is the same as for the normal duple pattern, the conductor thinking 4-5. A steady rhythmic pulse must be maintained throughout this uneven pattern.

Figure 25.1 The Five Pattern (3 + 2)

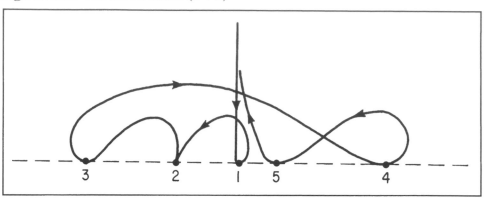

Figure 25.2 The Five Pattern (2 + 3)

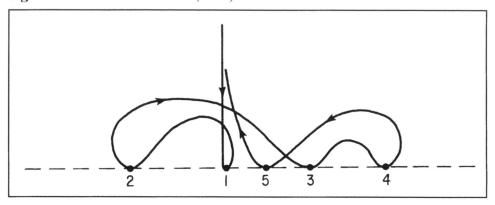

Figure 25.3 The Seven Pattern (3 + 4)

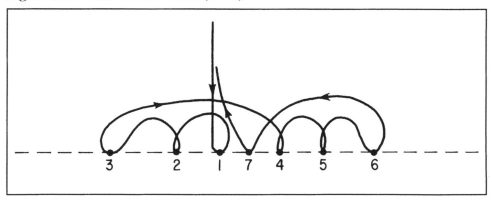

A slow meter of seven can be conducted in one of two ways, depending upon the rhythmical organization of the meter: 3 + 4 or 4 + 3. Figure 25.3 shows the diagram of the gesture for seven when the rhythm is grouped 3 + 4. Notice that beats two and three move to the left of the vertical plane, and beats four, five, and six move to the right.

The 4 + 3 organization of the seven pattern is shown in Figure 25.4. Beats two, three, and four move to the left of the vertical plane, while beats five and six move to the right. In both diagrams, beat seven is in the same position on the horizontal plane.

Figure 25.4 The Seven Pattern (4 + 3)

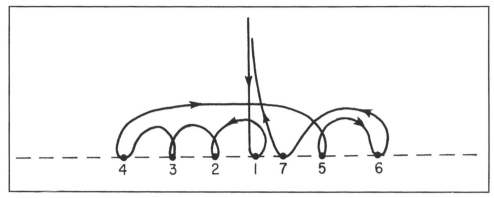

When the tempo of the music in seven meter moves fast, the pattern reverts to triple, with one of the three beats "dragging" or longer. In the fast seven meter, the rhythmic organization can be one of three ways: 3 + 2 + 2, 2 + 3 + 2, or 2 + 2 + 3. In each of the cases, the gesture containing the three pulses becomes the drag beat. Again, the conductor must maintain a steady pulse throughout the uneven pattern.

Other asymmetric meters such as nine, ten, and eleven are less common, and are used more with fast tempos. The patterns for these meters are usually some type of the three, four, or five patterns, with the underlying beats grouped again according to the rhythmic organization.

CHANGING METERS

Contemporary music often uses changing meters in which the music shifts from one meter to another (Example 25.1). In most cases, the conductor determines the basic beat note and keeps it steady when shifting the pattern from two to three to five, and so forth. If there is to be a change in the beat note, the composer most often will indicate such a change in the score itself, notating, for example, that the previous quarter-note pulse is now equal to a half-note pulse.

Sometimes asymmetrical meters are found interspersed among simple meter patterns. In Example 25.2, the basic pulse is the quarter note, but the 3/8 measure has an extra half pulse that does not fit logically into a conducting pattern. In this case, the 3/8 measure is conducted with a three pattern at twice the tempo, maintaining the eighth-note division. Because this is a quick movement, the three pattern is best conducted from the wrist only. When the tempo is fast, however, such a quick movement is almost impossible to make clear. Therefore, the 3/8 measure is conducted

Example 25.1 Changing Meters: Constant Pulse

Example 25.2 Changing Meters: Changing Pulse

in one, like a "drag" beat in asymmetric patterns. Care must be taken that the three eighth pulses are not conducted as a triplet.

GUIDED PRACTICE

1. Practice in unison as the instructor models each of the asymmetric patterns in Figure 25.1–25.4.

2. Practice in unison as the instructor models the five and seven patterns at a fast tempo using "drag" beats.

3. Conduct the changing meter patterns in Examples 25.1 and 25.2. Vary the tempo in Example 25.2 from slow to fast. For the slow tempo use a quick three pattern from the wrist; the fast tempo requires that the 3/8 measure be conducted in one with a "drag" beat.

4. Review the right hand six pattern for *Silent Night,* practicing in unison with the instructor.

5. Review the left hand gestures for *Silent Night,* and practice in unison.

6. Practice *Silent Night* with ambidextrous conducting.

7. Review and practice the slow nine and twelve patterns, as well as the slow asymmetric patterns of five and seven.

ASSIGNMENT

1. Practice *Silent Night* for individual conducting and Videotaping #7 in the next class session.

2. Practice the slow five, seven, nine, and twelve patterns for individual conducting in the next class session.

3. Read Lesson 26 in preparation for the next class session.

Lesson 26

■ Videotaping #7

Conducting a selection as simple as *Silent Night* may appear to be easy, but executing a smoothly flowing line and subtle ictus takes much practice.

Objectives for this seventh videotaping lesson are

- habitual posture and arm/hand positioning
- preparatory set with clear preparatory gesture, rhythmic breathing motion, and eye contact
- clear patterns when conducting meters in five, six, seven, nine, twelve
- independent use of right and left hands
- a meaningful interpretation

Preparation

The main objective of this videotaping is ambidextrous conducting. Coordination between hands should be more natural. The conducting of compound and asymmetric meter patterns, while not a major objective of this course, also will be evaluated.

Review the elements that will be evaluated in this seventh videotaping as found on Evaluation Form VII in this lesson. This will serve as a review of all gestures and techniques studied thus far. Review the videotape of your conducting and follow the directives as to the use of the form. Pay close attention to the constructive comments made by your instructor on the tape, which will help you to complete the self-evaluation form.

As in previous taping session, when it is your turn to conduct proceed to the conductor's stand, place your music on it, and fix the tempo in your mind *before* raising your head and arm. Once you are set to begin, raise your head and arm simultaneously, scan the group with your eyes, give the preparatory gesture with rhythmic breathing motion, and keep your eyes up on the downbeat. *Silent Night* will be conducted first, followed by the conducting of patterns in five, seven, nine, and twelve.

If something goes wrong with your conducting at the very beginning, stop and begin again. If you lose your place or the pattern falters during the music—keep going!

Lastly, try to communicate each musical example. Ask yourself, "What is the character of *Silent Night,* and how can this be communicated?" No matter how good your technique is, you will be unconvincing if you do not convey the meaning and mood of the piece.

When it is someone else's turn to conduct, be a good ensemble member. Respond to the person conducting, sing or play out, and follow the tempo given. Support the conductor as an actively participating ensemble member. You will appreciate the same support when it is your turn.

GUIDED PRACTICE

1. Warm up with group practice of *Silent Night.*

2. Review the five, seven, nine, and twelve patterns.

3. Now is the time to ask any last-minute questions.

VIDEOTAPING #7—*SILENT NIGHT* (Gruber)—FIVE, SEVEN, NINE, TWELVE PATTERNS

ASSIGNMENT

1. View Videotaping #7, complete Evaluation Form VII on both sides, and turn it in to the instructor.

2. Continue the practice of all elements of ambidextrous conducting. *Silent Night* will appear again on the final conducting exam.

3. Read Lesson 27 in preparation for the next class session.

Name _____ Date ___/___/___ [ ][|]
                                                          Grades

EVALUATION FORM VII

Complete the self-evaluation below. Leave those elements blank that are basically correct; use + for very good elements and − for elements that need improving.

Posture—Arm/Hand Positioning

_____ posture   _____ arm/hand positioning

Preparation

_____ mental set   _____ correct tempo

_____ group scan   _____ correct dynamic level

_____ smooth preparatory gesture   _____ correct articulation

_____ rhythmic breathing motion   _____ clear ictus

_____ eye contact   _____ confident and assuring demeanor

Patterns and Releases

_____ vertical plane   _____ pattern clarity: nine

_____ horizontal plane   _____ pattern clarity: twelve

_____ pattern clarity: five   _____ internal releases

_____ pattern clarity: six   _____ final release

_____ pattern clarity: seven   _____ communication

Baton Grip and Use

_____ proper contact points   _____ baton on vertical plane

_____ natural curve of fingers   _____ ictus at baton tip

_____ correct direction of baton   _____ ictus on horizontal plane

Left Hand

_____ at-rest position: side   _____ appropriate dynamics

_____ at-rest position: front   _____ crescendo-decrescendo

_____ attention position   _____ appropriate releases

_____ smooth and independent   _____ sustaining gestures

Evaluation Summary. Summarize your conducting evaluation in narrative form. Write one paragraph summarizing the positive elements of your conducting and one paragraph on those elements that need improving.

199

Summarize positive elements:

Summarize those elements in need of improvement:

Lesson 27

- Accents
- Tempo Alterations
- Section Cues

The techniques to be learned in this lesson are more advanced, and you will need to spend additional practice time in learning to master them.

Objectives for this lesson are
- learning to conduct accents
- learning to make secure tempo alterations
- section and/or solo cueing
- a review of terminology

ACCENTS

The dynamic accent (>, *sfz.*) must be visible to the ensemble in the conductor's gesture, which begins with the preparation leading to the accented beat. The preparatory ictus is the beat or "and" of the beat (in slower tempos) immediately before the accent. This gesture must be larger than the normal ictus or rebound to indicate the dynamic change that is about to take place on the accent. For a forceful accent, it is helpful for the conductor to pause ever so briefly after the preparation and before the stroke on the accented beat. This "space" between preparation and accent communicates the expectancy of the accent. The gesture for the accented beat itself is matched to the degree of the desired force.

The left hand can be used to make an accent even more dramatic. In this case, the left hand mirrors the right for the preparation and accent; the left hand should not continue to mirror the pattern following the accent.

GUIDED PRACTICE

1. Practice the exercise in Example 27.1 with the right hand only. Change the beat on which the accent occurs for each repetition.

2. Add the left hand to the right for the exercise in Example 27.1, being sure not to mirror the pattern following the accented beat.

Example 27.1 Conducting Accents

TEMPO ALTERATIONS

Changes in tempo during the course of conducting must be clearly communicated to the ensemble. In general, a slowing of the tempo requires larger gestures, while an increasing of the tempo uses smaller gestures. For the *ritardando,* the pattern expands, while the size of the pattern decreases for the *accelerando.*

Adding the left hand to the tempo change is a good way of signaling the ensemble that a change is taking place. The left hand may be added a beat or two prior to the tempo change to prepare the musicians, and it mirrors the right hand throughout the change in tempo.

The *ritardando* requires deliberate, larger conducting motions, depending upon the breadth of the ritard. A feeling of dragging the hand or baton will convey the slowdown. However, the *accelerando* requires conducting motions that become ever smaller as the pace of the music increases. For very fast tempos, there is little time for movement between beats.

The *tenuto* is a type of tempo change in that it requires a stretching or "mini-hold" of the note on which it occurs. This gesture is similar to that used for the no-break fermata, except the hold is more of a stretch. A slight drag of the beat is useful for conducting the *tenuto,* and is accomplished by turning the hand at the wrist in the opposite direction from which the arm is moving. In Example 27.2, the *tenuto* on beat three would be indicated by the arm moving (stretching) to the right with the hand/baton turned inward to the left. When the *tenuto* beat moves on, the hand/baton moves quickly to the right before moving inward for beat three. This is a subtle gesture and, depending upon the tempo, may be executed very quickly.

GUIDED PRACTICE

1. Practice the exercise in Example 27.2 using the right hand/baton only. Practice at different tempos.

2. Practice the exercise in Example 27.3 using both right and left hands. Change the beat on which the ritard begins for each repetition.

3. Practice the exercise in Example 27.4 using both right and left hands. Change the beat on which the *accelerando* begins for each repetition.

Example 27.2 Conducting Tenuto

Example 27.3 Conducting Ritardando

Example 27.4 Conducting Accelerando

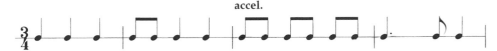

SECTION CUES

Up to now, cueing has been used only for the entire ensemble. There are many times, however, when the conductor needs to cue one section or one member. This type of cue is similar to the full ensemble cue, but the gesture is placed in the direction of the member or section. Also, the cue is prepared and eye contact made at least one beat prior to the actual cue.

Cues may be made with the right hand/baton, left hand, or both when a double cue is necessary. When possible the cueing gesture should be given within the form of the conducting pattern. This maintains the place of each ictus and keeps the pattern clear. Therefore, a cue on beat one is given in an outward but downward direction. A cue on a leftward beat will be given outward and to the left, and a cue on a rightward beat will be outward and to the right. A cue on the last beat of a measure most often will be outward and downward with an immediate upward rebound to prepare for the next downbeat.

Cueing various sections or members requires that the conductor turn the body in the direction of the cue. The torso may be turned slightly or, for cues in more extreme directions to the left or right, one foot at a time may move one step in either direction. The left foot steps only left and the right foot only right. The feet never cross! Jumping around on the podium, as some conductors do, is distracting and to be avoided.

A problem occurs when cueing the right side of the ensemble on a leftward beat with the right hand/baton. Because the cue is given from a right-to-left direction, the body and arm must be turned right before the leftward cue is given. This position will permit the leftward cue to go outwards to the section or member because the entire conducting area has been moved to the right.

The same problem occurs when the left hand is cueing the left side of the ensemble on a rightward beat. By turning to the left, the conductor can cue the rightward beat in such a way as to move it outward to the ensemble while maintaining the integrity of the pattern.

There are five basic cueing areas for the ensemble as shown in Figure 27.1. Cues to sections two and three need to be on a higher plane to indicate the cue is being directed to people in the back of the ensemble. Cues to sections one and four are at the level of the horizontal plane or slightly lower, and cues to section five are on the level of the horizontal plane or slightly higher.

Figure 27.1 Cueing Planes

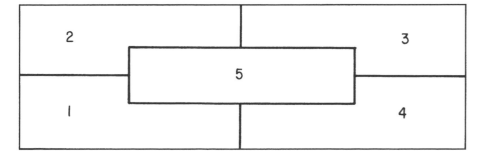

Cueing may be done with the left hand only, especially when the right hand/baton is needed to maintain a strict pattern. Care must be taken that cues from the left hand do not cross over the right hand/baton, especially when cues are given on the right side. In this case, the conductor must face more to the right in the direction of the cue.

Cues are given beyond the regular conducting area for emphasis and visibility. When only the left hand is cueing, it should move out farther than the right hand/baton. If both hands are used to cue, both move outward in the direction of the section or member being cued.

The move outward for the cue begins with the beat preceding the cue. Eye contact is made at the same time or sooner. A conductor cannot wait to begin the cue *on* the cue, or the gesture will be late and jerky. The cue itself is given with a slight pulsing action of the arm/hand to give emphasis to the entrance. The amount of pulse is in relation to the dynamic level and articulation desired.

The left hand position for cueing is generally with palm open to the right, fingers extended forward (never completely straight), and thumb up. Sometimes a conductor will use only the first finger to cue an individual. Entrances at a soft dynamic level may be indicated with the palm facing downward, and loud dynamic levels may be cued with palm upward for greater contrast.

The amount of cueing a conductor does is related to the needs of the ensemble. Generally, less experienced groups need more cues, and vice versa. However, even the most experienced ensemble players who have not been playing for numerous measures are reassured when the conductor cues their entrance.

Sometimes a cue can be given with just a nod of the head. In this case, lifting the head prior to the nod serves as the preparatory gesture. Good eye contact must be maintained, and the section or person being cued must be close enough to see this gesture. In general, this type of cue is better reserved for conducting smaller, chamberlike ensembles.

GUIDED PRACTICE

1. Draw Figure 27.1 with its five ensemble sections on the chalkboard. Using the four pattern and quarter-note movement in common time, practice cueing each of the sections in succession on beat one with the right hand/baton. Then cue each section on beats two, three, and four. Monitor for the proper elevation of the cueing plane.

2. Practice cueing as above with the left hand only. Be sure to turn the body when necessary.

3. Practice cueing as above with the right hand/baton keeping the pattern and the left hand giving the cues. Monitor for any hand crossing.

"The Handsome Butcher" (from *Three Hungarian Folksongs*) by Matyas Seiber

"The Handsome Butcher" (Example 27.5) is the last musical example to be studied in class. It is written for four-part chorus, and instruments double the vocal parts (Example 27.5a). It is a short selection, but has been chosen because it contains a tremendous number of challenges for the conductor. It will require much study and practice, and will be conducted as part of the final conducting exam.

The first section (measures 1–18) is presented for study in this lesson. The tempo is marked *Allegretto* ($\bullet = 138$), which is rather fast. The meter is duple, the dynamic level begins loud, and the articulation begins *marcato,* changing to *staccato* for the tenor part in measures seven and eight. Soprano, alto, and tenor entrances are cued successively in measures one–three, and five–eight. A double cue to soprano and alto in measure nine is marked *leggiero* (lightly). The tenor is cued in measure ten and all parts cadence in measures twelve and thirteen with a slight heaviness (*poco pesante*) and two final accents. Soprano and alto begin again in measure fourteen, this time *a tempo* and *piano.* The tenor enters in measure fifteen and the three parts

cadence again, this time *poco pesante,* but ending with two beats with *tenuto* markings. The cutoff is a final two-hand release on beat two. All of these markings should be noted in the score.

A measure-by-measure conducting analysis for each hand follows for section 1. The numbers in the left column correspond to the measure numbers. The sooner you memorize these eighteen measures, the faster your conducting skills will develop.

Section 1—*Allegretto* (♩ = 138)—*Forte—Marcato*

0—LH indicates *forte* with palm up; RH gives *marcato* preparation
1—LH cues soprano on beat one; RH conducts duple pattern, *marcato*
2—LH cues alto on beat one; RH conducts duple pattern; *marcato*
3—LH cues tenor on beat one; RH conducts duple pattern, *marcato*
4—LH at attention; RH conducts duple pattern, *marcato*
5—LH cues soprano; RH conducts pattern
6—LH cues alto; RH conducts pattern
7—LH cues tenor and mirrors RH for *staccato* articulation
8—LH and RH cueing tenor with *staccato* pattern
9—LH cues soprano; RH cues alto; smaller pattern and "lightly"
10—LH cues tenor; RH conducts pattern
11—LH at attention; RH conducts pattern
12—LH mirrors RH; larger motion (*poco pesante*); accent on two
13—LH mirrors RH accent on 1; hands stop for cut; hands prep *a tempo*
14—LH cues soprano; RH cues alto; smaller pattern (*piano*)
15—LH cues tenor; RH conducts pattern
16—LH turns page (early); RH conducts pattern
17—LH mirrors RH larger motion (*poco pesante*); *tenuto* (drag beat two inward)
18—LH mirrors RH *tenuto* on beat one (drag outward); final cut in both hands on beat two

GUIDED PRACTICE

1. Circle the notes for each cue in section 1 of "The Handsome Butcher."

2. Observe the instructor model section 1 of "The Handsome Butcher," each phrase separately (4 + 4 + 5 + 5) for each hand, and practice together.

Example 27.5 "The Handsome Butcher" from *Three Hungarian Folksongs.*

M. Seiber

Example 27.5a Instrumental Parts for "The Handsome Butcher"

ASSIGNMENT

1. Review the following sections for a final quiz on all of these materials: Using the Metronome (Lesson 2); Tempo Terminology (Lesson 4); Dynamics (Lesson 6); Character Terminology (Lesson 8); Accent, Articulation, and Connecting Terms (Lesson 10); Repeat Markings (Lesson 18); Alto and Tenor Clefs (Lesson 20); C and B-flat Transpositions (Lesson 22); F, E-flat, and Other Transpositions (Lesson 24).

2. Review and practice the gestures for accents, tempo alterations, and sectional cues.

3. Begin practice of the first section of "The Handsome Butcher." Memorize the phrase structure (4 + 4 + 5 + 5). Study what is happening in each measure for each hand. Practice each hand separately and together.

4. Read Lesson 28 in preparation for the next class session.

Lesson 28

■ Conducting Synthesis 1

All of the techniques that you have learned previously now come together in conducting a rather challenging musical selection.

Objectives for this lesson are
- executing secure tempo and dynamic changes
- cueing sections accurately
- demonstrating changes in meter
- independent and confident use of left and right hands
- varied articulation changes including accents

GUIDED PRACTICE

Review with the instructor section 1 of "The Handsome Butcher" for all conducting gestures, and conduct together.

"The Handsome Butcher"—Section 2

Section 2 of "The Handsome Butcher" begins at measure 19; the tempo is marked "Tempo I," which is *allegretto*. All voices begin *forte* with *marcato* articulation. Notice that the bass part is doubly marked with accents, and special attention will be paid to this part in measures 19 and 20. An internal cutoff occurs on the second beat of measure 22, and all parts enter again in measure 23, with the tenor and bass parts marked with accents. Another internal release appears in measure 26. Notice the *meno f* indication in measure 27; this requires the "hot touch" gesture on beat one. An internal cutoff in measure 31 is followed by an immediate dynamic drop to *piano* in measure 32. The *poco rit.* is prepared with both hands on the first beat of measure 35, and the larger motions continue through beat one of measure 36, followed by an internal release with both hands. A measure-by-measure conducting guide follows.

Section 2—Tempo I—*Forte*—*Marcato*

18—LH up in prep to cue bass; RH up for preparatory gesture
19—LH cues bass on accents and mirrors RH pattern (*marcato*)
20—LH cues bass on accents and mirrors RH pattern (*marcato*)
21—LH at attention; RH conducts pattern
22—LH at attention; RH conducts beat one and internal release on two
23—LH cues bass and mirrors RH cue of tenor (*marcato*)
24—LH cues bass and mirrors RH cue of tenor (*marcato*)
25—LH at attention; RH conducts pattern
26—LH at attention; RH conducts beat one and internal release on two
27—LH indicates *meno f* with hot touch on beat one; RH on pattern
28–30—LH lowers to waist; RH conducts pattern slightly smaller
31—RH conducts beat one and internal cutoff on two; LH at attention
32–34—LH indicates *piano*; RH conducts smaller pattern
35—LH mirrors RH prep of *poco rit.* on beat one, and larger prep on two
36—LH mirrors RH *ritard* (larger beat) and two-hand cutoff on two

GUIDED PRACTICE

> Conduct with the instructor section 2 of "The Handsome Butcher," reviewing all conducting gestures.

"The Handsome Butcher"—Section 3

Section 3 of "The Handsome Butcher" begins at measure 37; the tempo is marked *Piu pesante* (♩ = 104), which is heavier and slower. All parts are marked *forte,* with heavy accents.

A heavy two-hand preparation cues all entrances in measure 37. Notice the accented *staccato* on beat one in measure 40. This is executed by opening the left hand as it rises on beat two of measure 39, and closing it quickly on the downbeat of measure 40 with no rebound of either hand. Both hands prepare measure 41 on beat two of measure 40 by lifting straight up with power. The same gestures are used for measures 41–44 as for 37–40. However, the new tempo of *Presto* (♩ = 104) must be set for measure 45 with the lifting motion of the hands on beat two of measure 44. This is the identical gesture used in measure 40, but this time the lift must be very small to indicate the change in dynamics to *pp.*

Measures 45–49 move one beat to the measure in the right hand/baton. The tempo of 104 for the quarter note now becomes the same tempo for the half note, which means that the music is moving twice as fast. The preparation for the tempo change in measure 44 is still at 104, but it now represents the half note, not the quarter

note. When the tempo changes in measure 45, one pulse now represents a whole measure, where earlier (measures 37–44), one pulse represented half a measure.

The left hand in measures 45–49 should indicate *pianissimo* (palm down). Also, the posture may be slightly crouched to indicate a very soft dynamic level. There is a two-hand release on beat two of measure 49.

Notice the *fermata* over the bar line in measure 49. This indicates a "long break." Therefore, a new two-handed preparatory gesture must be given for the entrances at measure 50.

The pulse reverts to the quarter note in measure 50, with the tempo indication *Allegretto moderato* (♩ = 112), or slower. The dynamic level comes up to *mf,* and the left hand turns palm upward to indicate this on the downbeat. Posture returns to normal (standing tall) to emphasize the dynamic change. There is another two-hand internal release in measure 51, followed by another fermata over the bar line. A new two-hand preparation is needed for measure 52; the left hand returns to indicating *mf* on the downbeat of measure 52 and the right hand/baton conducts the pattern.

The *ritardando* in measure 53 is prepared by both hands by exaggerating the motion on beat one, followed by large in–out drag motions for the *tenuto* on beat two of measure 53 and beat one of measure 54. A final cutoff in both hands concludes the composition. A measure-by-measure conducting analysis follows.

Section 3—*Piu Pesante* (♩ = 104)—*Forte—Marcato*

36—LH mirrors RH for *marcato* preparatory gesture

37–39—LH mirrors RH on strong *marcato* pattern

40—LH closed-fist release on beat one (*staccato)*; RH conducts beat one but does not rebound; both hands lift strongly to prep measure 41

41—LH mirrors RH on strong *marcato* pattern

42—LH turns page (early); RH conducts strong *marcato* pattern

43—LH mirrors RH on strong *marcato* pattern

44—LH closed-fist release on 1 (*staccato*); RH conducts beat one but does not rebound; both hands lift a little to prep measure 45 *pp*

45–48—*Presto* (♩ = 104), *rapido, pp*; LH indicates *pp*; RH conducts pattern lightly in one

48—LH/RH preparation circles for cutoff

49—LH/RH cutoff (final) on beat one; *fermata* (long break); two-hand preparatory gesture for measure 50

50—*Allegro moderato* (♩ = 112); LH palm up for *mf*; RH conducts pattern

51—LH/RH prep cutoff with circle on beat one; subdivide release on two *fermata* (long break); two-hand prep for measure 52

52—LH palm up for *mf*; RH conducts pattern

53—LH mirrors larger RH motion to prepare *ritard.* on beat one, with inward, slow drag motion (*tenuto*) on two

54—LH mirrors RH on outward drag motion on beat one, followed by mirrored final release on two. *Fine!*

GUIDED PRACTICE

> Observe as the instructor models section 3 of "The Handsome Butcher" for all conducting gestures, and conduct together.

ASSIGNMENT

1. Practice the conducting of all three sections of "The Handsome Butcher." Practice each hand separately and combined.

2. Review *O Beautiful for Spacious Skies* (or "Break Forth, O Beauteous Heavenly Light") and *Silent Night* for the final conducting exam.

■ Conducting Synthesis 2

You now have a vocabulary of basic techniques with which to conduct, and you should be able to apply these gestures to untutored compositions.

Objectives for this lesson are
- studying an untutored musical selection for conducting
- reviewing all conducting techniques
- preparing for the final conducting exam

"Alleluia" (from *Uns ist ein Kind geboren*) by J. Kuhnau

There are four selections on the final conducting exam, one of which, the "Alleluia" from a cantata formerly attributed to J. S. Bach (Example 29.1), will not be taught to you in class. At this point in your development, you should be able to take the skills learned and transfer them to a piece of music for which you have received no instruction.

The tempo is traditionally taken at *allegro*. You will have to determine the speed in relation to the clean articulation of the sixteenth notes. It is advisable to take the tempo at a reasonable speed. The meter is triple, and the dynamic level is probably *mf* throughout.

As in the past, your right hand/baton should be used to conduct the orchestra. The left hand is used to conduct the chorus parts, which are straightforward and need little more than entrances and releases. You may wish to use some sustaining gestures with the left hand.

There are two passages of hemiola in the vocal parts: measures 21–22, and 36–37. Decide how you want to conduct these measures.

A *ritardando* is implied for the last two measures. This is typical of Baroque style and you will need to practice conducing a clear, smooth ending.

Example 29.1 "Alleluia" from *Uns ist ein Kind geboren*   **J. Kuhnau**

Breathe for cues

Final

Example 29.1a Instrumental Parts for "Alleluia"

GUIDED PRACTICE

1. Practice conducting section 1 of "The Handsome Butcher."
2. Review again with the instructor the conducting gestures for sections 2 and 3 of "The Handsome Butcher."
3. Practice all three sections of "Butcher" in succession, pausing very briefly between sections.

ASSIGNMENT

1. Practice "The Handsome Butcher" for individual conducting and Videotaping #8 in the next class session.
2. Begin to study the "Alleluia" for conducting on the final exam.
3. Review and practice *O Beautiful* or "Break Forth" and *Silent Night* for the final conducting exam.
4. Read Lesson 30 in preparation for the next class session.

Lesson 30

■ Videotaping #8

This is your last individual conducting before the final exam. All of the elements studied in this course now come together for a polished performance.

Objectives for this lesson are
- proper posture and arm/hand positioning
- preparatory set and clear preparatory gesture
- eye contact and rhythmic breathing motion
- clear patterns, cues, and releases
- independent use of left and right hands
- proper use of the conducting baton
- appropriate dynamic, articulation, tempo, and sustaining gestures
- confident and assuring leadership
- communication that effectively interprets the music

Preparation

Read the elements that will be evaluated in this last videotaping as found on Evaluation Form VIII in this lesson. This will serve as a final review of all gestures and techniques studied in the course.

When it is your turn to conduct, proceed to the conductor's stand, place your music on it, and fix the tempo in your mind *before* raising your head and arm. Once you are set to begin, raise your head and arm simultaneously, scan the group with your eyes, give the preparatory gesture with rhythmic breathing motion, and keep your eyes up on the downbeat. If something goes wrong with your conducting at the beginning, stop and begin again. If, however, you lose your place or the pattern falters during the music—keep going!

Lastly, try to communicate the spirit of the musical example. "The Handsome Butcher" (Example 27.5) is a fun, nonsense piece, and you should have fun with it. Much of your final conducting exam grade will be based upon how well you communicate the music.

GUIDED PRACTICE

> 1. Warm up with group practice of "The Handsome Butcher."
> 2. Ask any last-minute questions at this point.

VIDEOTAPING #8—"THE HANDSOME BUTCHER" (Seiber)

ASSIGNMENT

1. View Videotaping #8, complete Evaluation Form VIII on both sides, and return it to the instructor at the final exam time.
2. Practice the four selections for the final conducting exam: *O Beautiful for Spacious Skies* or "Break Forth, O Beauteous Heavenly Light," *Silent Night,* "The Handsome Butcher," and "Alleluia." (Your instructor may choose to substitute other musical examples before the final exam.)

Name _____   Date ____/____/____   ┌─────┬─────┐
                                                                    │   │   │
                                                                    └─────┴─────┘
                                                                       Grades

EVALUATION FORM VIII

Complete the self-evaluation below. Leave those elements blank that are basically correct; use + for very good elements and − for elements that need improving.

Posture—Arm/Hand Positioning

_____ posture   _____ arm/hand positioning

Preparation

_____ mental set   _____ correct tempo

_____ group scan   _____ correct dynamic level

_____ smooth preparatory gesture   _____ correct articulation

_____ rhythmic breathing motion   _____ clear ictus

_____ eye contact   _____ confident and assuring demeanor

Patterns and Releases

_____ vertical plane location   _____ pattern clarity

_____ vertical plane amplitude   _____ internal releases

_____ horizontal plane location   _____ final release

_____ horizontal breadth   _____ release preparation

_____ clear ictus on each beat   _____ communication

Baton Grip and Use

_____ proper contact points   _____ baton on vertical plane

_____ natural curve of fingers   _____ ictus at baton tip

_____ correct direction of baton   _____ ictus on horizontal plane

Left Hand

_____ at-rest position: side   _____ appropriate dynamics

_____ at-rest position: front   _____ *crescendo-decrescendo*

_____ attention position   _____ appropriate releases

_____ smooth and independent   _____ sustaining gestures

Evaluation Summary. Summarize your conducting evaluation in narrative form. Write one paragraph summarizing the positive elements of your conducting and one paragraph on those elements that need improving.

A. Summarize positive elements:

B. Summarize those elements in need of improvement:

■ Coda

If you have mastered the techniques presented in this conducting method, you should now have a basic conducting vocabulary upon which to build your own personal style. However, the only real way to become an accomplished conductor is to practice the art regularly with an ensemble. Amateur groups abound, and you may wish to pursue a position with one to further develop your conducting technique.

Those of you who have found conducting particularly interesting and satisfying should consider taking at least one more course at the intermediate or advanced level. While the method in this book is generic in nature, there are specific techniques in working with choirs, bands, and orchestras that could not be covered in this course. Professional conductors need experience in all of these areas.

The conducting field has been dominated by men for centuries. It is encouraging, however, to find that more women are finding professional conducting positions. This author has noted in the teaching of conducting that women are equal to and often surpass men when it comes to expressive communication and leadership potential. Women who love to conduct should not be intimidated by this male-dominated field. Rather, they should pursue it vigorously, serving as models for future generations.

In his essay "On Conducting," the nineteenth-century composer Hector Berlioz writes:

> Among creative artists the composer is almost the only one depending upon a host of intermediates between him and the public—intermediates who may be intelligent or stupid, friendly or hostile, diligent or negligent. It is in their power to carry his work on to brilliant success or to disfigure, debase and even destroy it.
>
> Singers are often considered the most dangerous of these intermediaries; I believe that this is not true. In my opinion, the conductor is the one whom the composer has most to fear. A bad singer can spoil only his own part, but the incapable or malevolent conductor can ruin everything. A composer must consider himself happy if his work has not fallen into the hands of a conductor who is both incapable and hostile; for nothing can resist the per-

nicious influence of such a person. The most excellent orchestra becomes paralyzed, the best singers feel cramped and fettered, all energy and unity are lost. Under such direction the noblest and boldest inspirations can appear ridiculous, enthusiasm can be violently brought down to earth, the angel is robbed of his wings, the genius is transformed into an eccentric simpleton, the divine statue is plunged from its pedestal and dragged in the mud. Worst of all, when new works are performed for the first time, the public and even listeners endowed with the highest musical intelligence are unable to recognize the ravages perpetrated by the stupidities, blunders and other offenses of the conductor.*

Conducting is not for the weak! It is true, however, that conductors take on a great responsibility when they must interpret or bring to life another's composition. Such an act is not to be taken lightly, and requires much preparation. Hopefully, you will want to become the best musician possible in order to bring about the highest musical results. Study, commitment, and practice are the necessary ingredients. If you have what it takes, labor on! The world is in need of people who can inspire, lead, and produce that which ennobles humanity through artistic expression.

---

*Hector Berlioz, *Treatise on Instrumentation*. New York: Edwin F. Kalmus Music Publishers, 1948, p. 410.

■ Musical Examples Index

Anonymous
  My Country 'Tis of Thee, 55
  The Farmer in the Dell (excerpt), 172

Bach, J.S.
  "Air," from *Orchestral Suite No. 3 in
    D Major,* 163
  "Break Forth O Beauteous Heavenly
    Light," 144
Barnby, J., *Now the Day is Over,* 31
Beethoven, L. van
  "Ode to Joy" from *Symphony No. 9,*
    mov. 4, 57
  Theme from *Symphony No. 7,* mov. 2, 52
  "Turkish March" theme from *The Ruin
    of Athens,* 121
Billings, W., *Chester,* 32
Brahms, J., *Erlaube mir,* 97

Delibes, L., "Waltz" theme from
    Coppelia, 79
Dvorak, A., theme from *Slavonic Dance
    No. 10,* 65

Evans, D., "A Gaelic Melody," 187

Grieg, E.
  "Ase's Death" theme from *Peer Gynt,*
    Op. 46, No. 2, 128
  Theme from "In the Hall of the
    Mountain King," 42
Gruber, F., *Silent Night,* 185

Handel, G.
  "Hornpipe" from *Water Music,* 53
  "La Paix" from *Royal Fireworks Music,*
    188
  "Surely He Hath Borne Our Griefs"
    from *Messiah* (excerpt), 158
Haydn, J.
  Austrian Hymn, 35
  "Chorale St. Antonii" (formerly
    attributed to Haydn), 87
  Themes A & B from *Symphony No. 94,*
    mov. 3, 97

Kuhnau, J., "Alleluia" from *Uns ist ein
    Kind geboren* (formerly attributed to
    J.S. Bach), 218

Lisle, R. de, *La Marseillaise* (excerpt), 172

Morley, T., *Sing We and Chant It,* 81

Saint-Saëns, C., "Praise Ye the Lord of
    Hosts" from *Christmas Oratorio,* 100
Seiber, M., "The Handsome Butcher,"
    from *Three Hungarian Folksongs,* 206
Sibelius, J., theme from *Finlandia,* 139
Smith, J., *The Star-Spangled Banner,* 182
Strauss, J., theme from *Emperor Waltz,* 79

Ward, S., *O Beautiful for Spacious Skies,*
    140
Willis, R., *It Came Upon the Midnight
    Clear* (excerpt), 171

■ Topical Index

Accelerando, 202
Accents, 201–2
Accent terms, 90
Alto clef, 165–66
Amplitude, 25
Arm position, 13–15
Articulation, 17, 39–40
Articulation terms, 90
Asymmetric meters, 193–95

Baton grip, 67–70
Baton selection, 63–64
Breadth of plane, 25

Changing meters, 195–96
Character terminology, 71
Circle drill, 131–33
Class organization, 3
Clefs, 165–66
Communication, 2
Composer's intent, 167
Compound meters, 183–84
Connecting terms, 91
Course requirements, 4
Crescendo, 64, 86, 125–126
Cues, 157–60
     section, 203–4

Daily dozen, 54
Decrescendo, 64, 86, 125–27
Dynamic changes, 64
Dynamics terminology, 60–61

Entrances on incomplete beats, 170–72
Evaluation forms
     form I, 47–48
     form II, 75–76
     form III, 107–8
     form IV, 111–12
     form V, 153–54
     form VI, 177–78
     form VII, 199–200
     form VIII, 229–30
     midterm form, 115–16
Eye contact, 19

Fermatas, 179–81
Final release, 29–30
     beat two, 60
Five pattern, 193–94
Four pattern, 24–29

Hand position, 13–15
Hemiola, 156
Horizontal plane, 11–12
Hot touch, 128–29

Ictus, 15–16
Internal release, 29
     beat two, 60, 86, 92–93
Interpretation, 167–68

Left hand conducting, 119–33
     circle drill, 131–33
     crescendo, 125–26

decrescendo, 125–27
dynamic levels, 122–29
four positions, 129–30
"hot touch," 128–29
mirroring, 119–20
strengthening techniques, 147
sustaining gestures, 135–38
Legato, 39
Listener's response, 167–68
Long-break fermata, 179–80

Marcato, 39–40
Marking beats, 171
Melding of beats, 30
Metronome, 20–22
Midterm conducting exam
    part 1, 113–14
    part 2, 117–18

Nine pattern, 184
No-break fermata, 179–81

Objectives, 2–3, 5, 231–32
One pattern, 77–78

Pickup note entrance, 94
    incomplete beats, 170–72
Posture, 6–10
Preparatory gesture, 16–20

Rebound motion, 25
Release on one, 80
Repeat markings, 148–50
Rhythmic breathing motion, 19
Ritardando, 202

Seven pattern, 194–95
Short-break fermata, 179–81
Six pattern, 183
Staccato, 39
Subdivision, 155–57
Sustaining gestures, 135–38
    forward sweep, 137–38
    horizontal sweep, 136–37

Tempo alterations, 202–3
Tempo terminology, 42
Tenor clef, 165–66
Tenuto, 202
Three pattern, 49–50
Transpositions, 173–74, 191–92
    A transposition, 191
    B-flat transposition, 173–74
    C transposition, 173
    E-flat transposition, 191–92
    F transposition, 191
Twelve pattern, 184
Two pattern, 50–51

Vertical plane, 10–11